BEING A SUCCESS AT WHO YOU ARE

BEING A SUCCESS AT WHO YOU ARE

André Bustanoby

PYRANEE BOOKS

Zondervan Publishing House
Grand Rapids, Michigan

BEING A SUCCESS AT WHO YOU ARE

The fourth printing of *You Can Change Your Life* (copyright © 1976 by The Zondervan Corporation) was retitled BEING A SUCCESS AT WHO YOU ARE, copyright © 1985 by The Zondervan Corporation.

Pyranee Books are published by Zondervan
Publishing House, 1415 Lake Drive, S.E.,
Grand Rapids, Michigan 49506

Library of Congress Cataloging in Publication Data

Bustanoby, André.
    Being a success at who you are.
    Previously published as: You can change your personality. 1976. With new pref.
    Includes bibliographical references and indexes.
    1. Christian life—1960 2. Personality. 3. Conversion.
I. Title.
BV4501.2.B94   1984   248.4   84-11947
ISBN 0-310-45381-X

All rights reserved. No part of this publication may be reproduced, stored in a retrieval system, or transmitted in any form or by any means—electronic, mechanical, photocopy, recording, or any other—except for brief quotations in printed reviews, without the prior permission of the publisher.

Printed in the United States of America

Contents

Acknowledgments
Preface
1. LORD, CUT ME GENTLY *13*
2. IS YOUR PERSONALITY HURTING YOUR SPIRITUAL LIFE? *21*
3. WHAT IS PERSONALITY? *27*
4. GETTING A HANDLE ON YOUR PERSONALITY *33*
5. A MODEST PROPOSAL FOR CHANGE *51*
6. THE MANAGERIAL-AUTOCRATIC PERSONALITY *73*
7. THE COMPETITIVE-EXPLOITIVE PERSONALITY *85*
8. THE BLUNT-AGGRESSIVE PERSONALITY *97*
9. THE SKEPTICAL-DISTRUSTFUL PERSONALITY *109*
10. THE MODEST-SELF-EFFACING PERSONALITY *119*
11. THE DOCILE-DEPENDENT PERSONALITY *131*
12. THE COOPERATIVE-OVERCONVENTIONAL PERSONALITY *143*
13. THE RESPONSIBLE-HYPERNORMAL PERSONALITY *155*
    APPENDIX A: Learning Contract *163*
    APPENDIX B: Interpersonal Adjective Check List *164*
    APPENDIX C: Communication Workshop *166*
    Notes *168*
    Subject Index *170*
    Scripture Index *173*

Acknowledgments

GRATEFUL acknowledgment is expressed to the publishers for permission to quote from the following books:

Timothy Leary, *Interpersonal Diagnosis of Personality: A Functional Theory and Methodolory for Personality Evaluation.* Copyright © 1957 The Ronald Press Company, New York.

"Your Personality May Be Killing You," in *Reader's Digest* (August 1974): Excerpted with permission from the *National Observer*, copyright Dow Jones & Company, Inc. 1974.

Carl Mundinger, *Government In The Missouri Synod.* © 1947 by Concordia Publishing House. Used by permission.

Maxwell Maltz, M.D., *Psycho-Cybernetics.* © 1960 by Prentice-Hall, Inc. Published by Prentice-Hall, Inc., Englewood Cliffs, New Jersey.

Charles Caldwell Ryrie, *Balancing the Christian Life.* Copyright 1969 Moody Press, Moody Bible Institute of Chicago. Used by permission.

G. C. Berkhouwer, *Man: The Image of God.* Used by permission of the publisher, Wm. B. Eerdmans Publishing Co., Grand Rapids, Michigan.

Jay E. Adams, *The Christian Counselor's Manual.* Copyright 1973 by the author, published by Baker Book House Company and used by permission.

James Dobson, *Hide or Seek.* Copyright 1975 by Fleming H. Revell Company. Used by permission.

"Interpersonal Adjective Check List," designed by Rolfe La Forge and Robert Suczek, in *Journal of Personality,* published by Duke University Press. Used by permission.

Unless otherwise indicated, Scripture quotations are from the *King James Version* or paraphrased from that version. Other versions quoted in this volume are as follows:

The New American Standard Bible. © The Lockman Foundation 1960, 1962, 1963, 1968, 1971. Published by Creation House, Inc., Carol Stream, Illinois.

Charles B. Williams, *The New Testament in the Language of the People.* Copyright 1937 by Bruce Humphries, Inc. Copyright assigned 1949 to the Moody Bible Institute of Chicago. Published by Moody Press, Chicago.

Preface

OUR PERSONALITIES are what we are—the sum of the traits or characteristics that are uniquely us. Though most of us like who we are, we also recognize that we can improve on ourselves. This book was written to help us do just that. By identifying our personality type and those traits that enhance our personality, we are able to achieve a greater success at being who we are. We do this by strengthening the traits that make us more balanced and eliminating the traits that lead to extreme, and therefore unbalanced and destructive, behavior.

This book was written primarily to Christians. It may be, however, that the reader is not a Christian. The word *Christian* suggests identification with Jesus Christ. Christianity is not a lifestyle or adherence to a particular creed. It is identification with Jesus Christ, who said, "I am the way, and the truth, and the life; no one comes to the Father, but through Me" (John 14:6 NASB). To be a Christian means to rest wholly on Jesus Christ as the way of acceptance with God the Father. This resting on Him is an act of faith that results in something called "the new birth" (John 3:1–18). If your Christianity is still in doubt, you are urged to rest on Jesus Christ as the way to the Father.

Lord, Cut Me Gently

Chapter 1
Lord, Cut Me Gently

> I am the true Vine and my Father is the Vine Cultivator.... Every branch in me that bears fruit He prunes it that it might still bring forth more fruit.... By this is my Father glorified, that you bear much fruit, and so prove to be my disciples *(John 15:1,2,8 NASB)*.

THIS PASSAGE of Scripture kept running through my mind. I did not realize its significance then in the fall of 1967, but I would in due time.

When I graduated from Dallas Theological Seminary in 1961, God blessed me with a wonderful congregation in my first pastorate. And I felt that my ministry was fruitful. Now for some reason, six years later, I was not wholly satisfied. I didn't understand this: I had no reason to be dissatisfied with the church. Night after night I would walk the streets of Arlington, Virginia, praying, "God, I feel dissatisfied, and I don't know why. I know that I'm bearing fruit, but I want to bear my maximum."

It was almost as though God spoke audibly. Clearly the words of Jesus in John 15 ran through my head. I understood them. I was linked to Jesus Christ in a union as intimate as a branch in a vine. This union occurred March 28, 1948, when I rested my hope for eternal life in Jesus Christ who calls Himself The Way, The Truth, and The Life. I also understood that by resting in that position I would be a fruit-bearing Christian because Jesus wanted to produce the fruit through me. I understood that God the Father had an important role in the process. Part of that role was to cut or prune the branches to maximize fruit bearing. I realized that mere random activity on the part of a vine does not assure it will bear the maximum amount of fruit; a vine needs to be cut back.

As I write these words I find it a bit frightening to note that the apostle John writes in the Greek present tense. He is saying in essence, "Every branch in Me that bears fruit He *repeatedly* prunes it that it might bring forth more fruit." As I look back over the pruning process of seven years, I silently pray a more intelligent prayer than I did in the fall of 1967. Now I say, "Lord, cut me gently."

That fall I really didn't know what this pruning was all about, though I had a fair understanding of Jesus' words. I remember so well talking to the Lord in the same bold way Peter did when he said, "Lord, I'll drink of that cup of suffering too!" Only my prayer was, "Lord, I don't know what this pruning is all about, but if that's what it takes to bear maximum fruit, lay it on me!"

My peripatetic prayer life continued into late fall. Repeatedly I asked God to do whatever pruning was necessary to bring about maximum fruit in my life. In November I received an invitation to candidate in a church in Southern California. To this ambitious young preacher the prospect of a large, well-staffed church in Southern California was a sweet morsel to consider. I felt that this kind of church was the badge of having arrived in the ministry. I certainly didn't say this at the time: this is said only in retrospect. When that thought crossed my mind, it was rationalized away. After all, this was an opportunity "to expand my field of service." It presented a greater and wider opportunity for "the Lord's work," and that must not be brushed aside.

Little did I know at that moment how my competitiveness and narcissism were feeding on the prospect of a move to Southern California. Ah, the poetic justice of it all. The narcissism and competitiveness that carried me to California were the very traits in my personality that God was to deal with there.

Am I saying that God was not in the move? Did the congregation that called me miss what God intended for them? No indeed! I and they were simply unaware of God's intention in the matter, and that was to answer my prayer for pruning and for them to learn something about themselves, which is another story that remains to be told. In fact, had I known the pain that was ahead, I would not have gone willingly.

When the Santa Ana winds are blowing from the desert, Southern California is beautiful in January. The air was eighty degrees, the palm trees were waving in the wind, but I could see snow on the mountains that ringed the Los Angeles basin. I felt I had arrived in the land of milk and honey in 1968.

The people were gracious, warm, and lively, and this was reflected in the life of the congregation. I settled down to my work with my usual vigor and enjoyed it immensely. The competitive-narcissist was being fulfilled.

Though I was enjoying my work at the church, something began to trouble me at home. My wife and I were drifting apart. I didn't understand it, and when we tried to talk about it, we usually wound up exchanging sharp words and breaking off into strained silence. Days passed in which we exchanged few words. Fay was obviously unhappy with me, but I couldn't understand why. Wasn't I doing everything right? Wasn't I providing for the family, spending time with them, and making them proud of me, God's devoted servant?

One morning I left for the office as usual, leaving Fay at the kitchen sink looking terribly unhappy. I closed my study door, sat down at my desk, put my head in my hands, and wept. What had gone wrong? I was hurt and confused. I prayed the kind of prayer Peter prayed when he tried to walk on the water — "Lord, help!" He answered. The Spirit said, "If you can't talk with Fay, try writing a letter."

The letter started, "Fay — You're destroying me." I poured out on paper all my resentment and frustration. Just as I was folding up the letter and trying to decide how and when to deliver it, Fay walked into the office.

"I just wrote you a letter," I said, and without thought of the timing I just handed it to her. She left with it and in about ten minutes returned. As she sat down she sighed and said, "We need help." We surely did need help! And in my typical take-the-bull-by-the-horns manner, I got on the phone.

Howard Hendricks was home. My former professor and good friend was the only one to whom I was willing to admit my failure. Was there any place in Southern California we could go for help? Yes, he replied. The American Institute of Family Relations (AIFR) in North Hollywood is nearby. It is not a Christian counseling service, but it is conservative in its outlook on marriage and the family.

It was tough to make that first appointment and tougher still to go with Fay and tell someone that our marriage was in trouble. But God bless Sam! What kindness and warmth our counselor showed as he took us into the consultation room. And when I discovered that he was a Conservative Baptist pastor working on his degree in counseling, I thought that he surely would understand me.

Yes, Sam understood me. He understood too well. With kindness and warmth he helped me understand what had gone wrong with my marriage: "You're giving Fay the message that you don't need her and that you are a self-sufficient person." Sam's analysis was the first glimmer of understanding about myself and what I was doing to hurt my marriage. But I was confused. Doesn't the Bible talk about strong leadership on the part of the husband and the submissiveness of the wife?

In the days that followed I tried to make Fay feel that I needed her. But God had only begun the pruning process. With

Lord, Cut Me Gently

Sam's encouragement I signed up for a two-week seminar at the institute. The seminar was for professional people working with families in the church and in government programs. The mornings were devoted to lectures, and the afternoons to something I had a strong reservation about — encounter groups. The press was carrying stories about the freaky things being done in groups, but I believed I was strong enough in the faith to weather any encounter.

I showed up for the first group dressed impeccably (my narcissistic one-upmanship) and with my usual air of assurance. They nailed me to the wall! For three hours a day, five days a week, they nailed me to the wall! Fifteen of my peers — pastors, chaplains, and social workers — nailed me! At first I thought, with typical spiritual rationalization, "These are unregenerate people. What do they know about spiritual things?" But I had trouble with this rationalization because they weren't faulting me for being spiritual. It was my attitude they didn't like — superior, sure of myself, and always right — yes, *always* right. I had an answer for everything, but they didn't want to hear me.

Crumbling inside, that's what it felt like. My world of security was being shaken; they weren't buying my security operation. I am verbal and can handle several people at once, but fifteen peers for three hours at a stretch was too much, even for me.

When I told Fay what they were saying about me, she nailed me too. "I've been telling you those things for years, but you won't listen. You always have to be right!" SMASH, BANG, POW, and all those other comic-book expletives! I didn't say a word, but the crumbling inside was turning into a major California mudslide. Quick, retreat! Shore up the defenses! But I have to go back tomorrow and face them again!

I lasted about a week, but could hold out no longer. I wanted to cry openly and tell everyone that I needed to appear strong and confident because I'm really not. So I held out until I got home. I wanted to tell Fay what was going on, but if I became weak, maybe she'd run all over me the way my dominant mother tried to do.

In the quiet of the bedroom that night, I broke. I told her of my fear of failure and fear of being dominated, especially by women. God bless Fay! She was warm and understanding. When I became weak, she didn't take advantage of me. She didn't make me feel small and incompetent. She listened with warmth and understanding, but she didn't emasculate me!

God's usual method of pruning is "by the Word spoken" (John 15:3). Godet puts it well in his commentary when he says,

> But if this means is not employed or is not sufficient, God makes use of other more grievous instruments, which, like a well-sharpened pruning knife, cut to the quick of the natural affections and carnal will.

That was 1970. And the cutting is still going on. God is still working on that competitive-narcissism. Afraid to be wrong? My world won't fall apart if I am. Need my wife, Fay? Yes, no longer am I the self-sufficient one. What the future holds, I don't know. But I do know this: it costs something to bear fruit. No, not the cost of compulsive service "in sacrifice doing the Lord's work." The idea of sacrifice must be tempered with Jesus' statement, "My yoke is easy and my burden is light." The cost I'm talking about is the hurt that comes through the pruning process. Don't be too quick to ask God to produce maximum fruit in you. And when you do ask Him, put a little P.S. on your prayer and say, "Lord, cut me gently."

*Is Your Personality
Hurting Your
Spiritual Life?*

Chapter 2
Is Your Personality Hurting Your Spiritual Life?

THE IDEA THAT a person's personality can hurt his spiritual life may seem strange to some. Yet if we gain a clear understanding of what personality and spirituality are, we will see that the idea is not so strange after all.

PERSONALITY DEFINED

Webster's defines personality as "the organization of the individual's distinguishing character, traits, attitudes or habits." Psychologists consider two factors in defining personality: recognizable unity and distinctive traits, drives, attitudes, and habits. We are interested in how a man functions as a whole person and how he is uniquely organized.

Whenever personality is discussed, it is treated almost as something sacred that must not be tampered with. The attitude is, "I am me, indelibly stamped by mysterious forces of life that cannot be changed, and what is more, to attempt to change me would be an act of sacrilege."

Such a view is nonsense in view of the fact that practically all human behavior is learned. Fortunately Freudian biological instinct and the tyranny of it are rapidly becoming a thing of the past. I am "me" with my unique unity and organization because I have *learned* to be this way over several decades. For seven years I have been discovering those elements of my personality that have been hindering my spiritual life and I am, with God's help, becoming a different person. And my life is richer and fuller because of this change.

Spirituality Defined

It may be asked how personality can hinder spiritual life. Is not the matter of spirituality purely one of the Spirit's operation whereby He overrules whatever is faulty about us?

Without question the Holy Spirit is preeminently involved in producing spirituality. But human responsibility is also a large factor. Charles Ryrie points up this truth in his book *Balancing the Christian Life*.[1] He shows the prominence of the human will in the spiritual life. It is true that we live the spiritual life by the power of the Son of God, but we nevertheless have the responsibility to live the life. *We* must make that choice.

Ryrie also warns against the kind of quietism abroad today in which Christians seem to refuse to take any responsibility for doing those things that are vital to spiritual and emotional growth. The slogan "let go and let God" is taken to the extreme where all human effort is seen as being "of the flesh."

When this attitude is carried over into interpersonal problems resulting from maladaptive personality traits, the same thing occurs. Everything is "spiritualized." God will "somehow" take care of the problem, and it is "prayed about" without thought being given to personal responsibility for the behavior or the correcting of it.

I have a responsibility to make right decisions and to behave myself. I cannot cop out of that responsibility by claiming to be a victim of my personality — as I have heard so often, "But that's the way I am." If my traits, drives, attitudes, and habits are contributing to my making wrong decisions and not behaving myself, then I better change them! If I as I am find it difficult to live the spiritual life, then perhaps I had better be someone else.

How we resist this! Why? Because we have that uneasy feeling that the fabric of our personality is in danger of being altered. Fear strikes deep into us that if we change, the organization of self will be thrown into utter chaos. Rather than permit the fabric of self to be altered, we resist. John Powell puts it well when he says,

> Sorry, but that is the way I am. . . . I was like this in the beginning, am now, and ever shall be . . . is a handy motto and delusion to have around if you don't want to grow up.[2]

Some Christians try to take an easier way out. They invoke the Spirit's help without understanding how He goes about helping us. They ask Him to change them and expect that God the Holy Spirit, like some kind of massive spiritual antibiotic, will correct whatever sickness in them is alienating them from wife, family, or friends.

The Spirit does not work that way. He pinpoints specific behavior that is counterproductive, requires us to acknowledge it, and only then purges it. In John 15 we are told of the role of the Father as the husbandman of the vine. He prunes *specifically* what needs to be pruned. But do we really want that pruning? I behave as I do because I feel most secure in that behavior. If the Spirit takes that behavior away, where does that leave me? I am afraid to surrender to the pruning process! I fight it!

Perhaps a personal illustration will help. A great impediment to my spiritual life has been a maladaptive expression of the Competitive-Exploitive Personality. I have always felt most secure in being right, winning, and being admired. When I was a small child I realized that if I appeared sure of myself and asserted myself, I could probably come out the winner. This worked even when I was *not* sure of myself!

Though I found a great deal of security in this behavior, it alienated others. One of the major causes of alienation was my need to be right. I could do mental gymnastics to justify myself, but I never stopped to consider that my self-justification was alienating others. When I did recognize what I was doing, I felt caught in a bind: if I attempted to prove I was right, I would alienate others; but if I didn't attempt to do this, I would feel terribly insecure. Indeed, I wouldn't come across to others as a competent, together person — the person I felt most secure being, or at least pretending I was. I held on to this alienating behavior because I thought I needed it for my security. I finally realized I had to be willing to give up what I thought I needed for feelings of security in order to improve my relations with others.

My point is that we often hang onto behaviors that alienate us from others because those behaviors lend us security. It is not just a matter of perversity or stubbornness that makes us hold on to counter-productive behavior. Our personality is often organized in a way that incorporates counterproductive behavior as part of its security operation.

When the Christian is put in this bind, he will rationalize and justify his behavior, and perhaps even quote Scripture in his defense. Why does he continue to alienate and not change? He does it because his personality is so organized as to make him feel secure with that behavior. The unique way in which your personality is organized *can* hinder your spiritual life.

What does a Christian do if this is so? Suppose you recognize that you are stubbornly hanging on to counterproductive behavior because you feel most secure with it? The following chapter takes a closer look at the phenomenon we call personality. We shall see that there is such a thing as "personality type" that functions in a predictable way. We will see further that the primary motivation for every personality type is the reduction of anxiety and promotion of self-worth. How we handle anxiety and low self-worth determines whether our personality is a spiritual liability or asset.

What Is Personality?

Chapter 3
What Is Personality?

IN THE PREVIOUS chapter personality was defined as "the organization of the individual's distinguishing character, traits, attitudes or habits." The two major elements of personality are *unity* and *distinctive traits*. I should add that we must be careful to distinguish between personality and character. Character involves moral judgments and the person's system of values. It is quite conceivable that a person may have a pleasing personality and an antichristian set of values. Likewise, a Christian may have a good set of values but a personality that alienates.

Over the years, psychologists have attempted to "type" personality, that is, to categorize all human beings as one kind of person or another. Various schemes have been offered.

One of the earlier attempts was that of Galen (A.D. 180) with his four humors: sanguine, phlegmatic, choleric, and melancholic. These humors, according to Galen, were the result of the secretions of various fluids in the body producing these humors.

Though Galen's system has been abandoned, it is recognized that the endocrine glands do have an influence on temperament. An overactive thyroid, for example, may produce nervousness, irritability, and insomnia. An underactive thyroid may bring about sluggishness. Endocrine secretions of the sex glands affect emotional interests. The pituitary, parathyroids, and adrenals affect temperament as does blood chemistry — acid-base balance, calcium-potassium ratio, and sugar tolerance. Endocrine function does not, however, offer a sufficient explanation for personality function.

The fallacy of the endocrine enthusiast is that he fails to distinguish between personality and temperament. Excitability has to do with temperament; the way it is handled has to do with personality. For example, the adrenal glands may secrete an excess of adrenalin. This will produce emotional excitement. One person may handle the excitement by becoming very talkative; another will handle it by becoming very quiet. The study of personality has to do not only with what people do, but also with why they do it.

Psychologists have attempted to use physique as a guide to explaining differences in personality. This view holds that bodily attributes reflect certain personality traits. Shakespeare was influenced by this thinking when he had Julius Caesar say,

> Let me have men about me that are fat; Sleek-headed men, and such as sleep o' nights; Yon Cassius has a lean and hungry look; He thinks too much: such men are dangerous (I,2).

Jung attempted to use introversion and extroversion as a method for typing personality. According to Jung, the introvert would live in the present and value his possessions and successes; the extrovert would live in the future and value his own standards and sentiments. The extrovert would be the practical man, and the introvert would be imaginative and intuitive.

Freud approached the matter of personality from the standpoint of instinct and man's relation to his instinctual past. We behave as we do, according to Freud, because of biological instinct and the thwarting of that instinct. He saw the influences of culture frustrating and impeding the natural development of personality. The shaping influence of culture was considered only in a negative way. Religion he considered a group neurosis, and art was analyzed as an expression of conflict in the artist's personality.

THE ROLE OF CULTURE

All these theories attempted to explain personality in terms of some internal unifying theme — structural or instinctual. In the past forty years psychologists have taken more seriously the place that culture plays in the shaping of personality. Interpersonal relations, the influence of people on people, has largely replaced Freud's overemphasis on biological forces at work in the personality. Leading thinkers in this movement have been Karen Horney, Harry Stack Sullivan, and Erich Fromm.

Karen Horney, author of *The Neurotic Personality*, maintained that neuroses originate in disturbed human relations. Erich Fromm in *Escape From Reason* places the cause of neurosis in the family; he says it is the human relations and not instinctual pressure that mold a personality. Psychiatrist Harry Stack Sullivan says that

> psychiatry is the study of processes that involve or go on between people. The field of psychiatry is the field of interpersonal relations under any and all circumstances in which these relationships exist.[3]

Sullivan, Horney, and Fromm all hold that the motive force of personality — that which makes us do what we do — is the avoidance of anxiety. More specifically, it is avoidance of anxiety that comes as a result of relations with other people. Anxiety is rooted in the dread expectation of derogation and rejection by others. It may be more accurate to look at it as a matter of *reducing* anxiety. A particular man behaves as he does (his personality expression) to reduce anxiety in his relations with other people.

Explaining personality in terms of reducing interpersonal anxiety helps explain why some people behave in ways that are bound to alienate. Why does a Christian husband belittle his wife and children and behave in an arrogant, selfish manner? Why is his personality marked with this typical alienating behavior in social relations and work? He is going through the process of reducing his anxiety. He is afraid that others may take advantage of him and make him feel like a worthless person. He reduces this anxiety by giving the message, "You better watch out how you behave toward me. I can be mean." By striking fear into the hearts of family and friends he reduces his anxiety. He believes that when others are afraid of him they won't give him trouble. True, he creates another problem: he alienates affection. But this problem provokes less anxiety than the anxiety of being overcome by family or co-workers. The behaviors that are used to reduce anxiety are called "security operations." As we shall see, they differ greatly from person to person. The different ways in which people employ security operations form the basis of typing personality.

Leary's Theory

Timothy Leary, following the work of Sullivan, Horney, and Fromm, has made an important contribution to the field of personality studies with his book *Interpersonal Diagnosis of Personality*, subtitled, "A Functional Theory and Methodology for Personality Evaluation" (The Ronald Press Company, New York, 1957). Leary wrote this book while he was Director of Psychology Research at the Kaiser Foundation Hospital in Oakland, California. Working under a grant from the United States Public Health Service and the Kaiser Foundation, Leary developed a system of personality evaluation based on the manner in which persons employ the interpersonal machinery of personality to ward off anxiety and preserve self-esteem. He saw all personalities as definable in eight types, each of them with an *adaptive* (balanced, and therefore successful in terms of human relations) and a *maladaptive* (unbalanced, and therefore unsuccessful in terms of human relations) expression.

Let's take a look, now, at how this system of typing personality works.

Getting A Handle on Your Personality

Chapter 4
Getting A Handle on Your Personality

THE INTERPERSONAL approach to personality is interested in how people relate to each other — what behaviors they engage in when they establish contact with another person. We use our personality to deal with others in a way that reduces our anxiety and preserves our feeling of self-worth. Remember that personality is defined as the unique way in which our behaviors are organized. They are organized as they are to promote self-worth and to reduce anxiety in our contacts with other people. These behaviors are called "security operations."

Security operations fall into two categories. First, we behave somewhere between absolute dominance and absolute submissiveness. By that I mean we feel most secure when we are either dominant or submissive or somewhere in between. Think of yourself as falling somewhere on the line as shown in Figure 1.

```
        100% Dominance
              ↑
              |
              |
              ↓
        100% Submissiveness
```
Figure 1

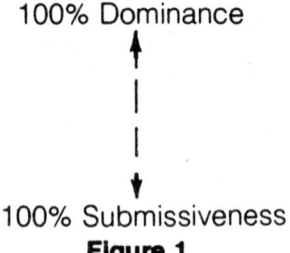

Some people feel most comfortable when they are being dominant, and others feel most comfortable when submissive. They use dominance or submissiveness to give them a feeling of security, and thus it is called a "security operation."

There is a second dimension to the security operation. We behave somewhere between 100 percent affection and 100 percent hostility. We feel most secure when we are either affectionate or hostile or somewhere in between. We choose the degree of affection or hostility we feel the most comfortable with and expect that posture to reduce our anxiety with respect to others. This dimension of the security operation is expressed in Figure 2.

100% Hostility ← — — — — — — → 100% Affection

Figure 2

When these security operations are put together, we have a two-dimensional scheme: (1) our behavior is somewhere along the dominant/submissive line, and (2) somewhere along the affectionate/hostile line (Figure 3).

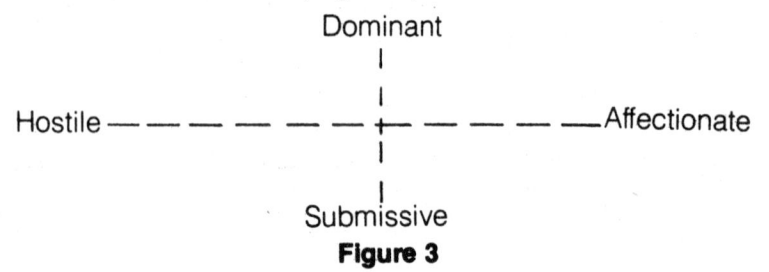

```
                  Dominant
                     |
                     |
    Hostile — — — — —+— — — — — Affectionate
                     |
                     |
                  Submissive
```
Figure 3

Getting a Handle on Your Personality 35

It is readily seen that this two-dimensional scheme of the security operation offers four combinations of behavior (Figure 4).

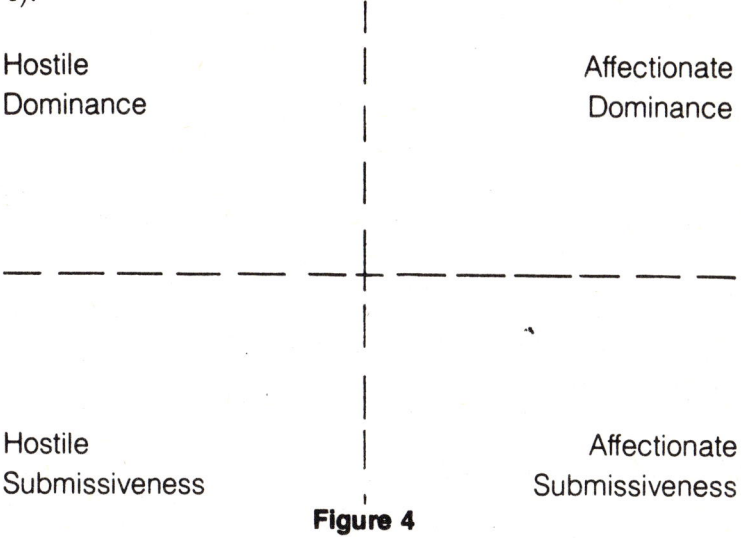

```
Hostile              |              Affectionate
Dominance            |              Dominance
                     |
                     |
                     |
─ ─ ─ ─ ─ ─ ─ ─ ─ ─ ─┼─ ─ ─ ─ ─ ─ ─ ─ ─ ─
                     |
                     |
Hostile              |              Affectionate
Submissiveness       |              Submissiveness
```
Figure 4

Behavior between people (interpersonal behavior) when viewed from this perspective follows fairly set patterns of interaction. Dominance and submissiveness hook each other in a push-pull relationship. Dominance pulls submissiveness, and submissiveness pushes itself toward dominance. Likewise, submissiveness pulls dominance on itself and dominance pushes itself on submissiveness.

Several other patterns of push-pull are predictable. Hostility and hostility engage in push-pull. So do affection and affection. Dominant-hostile behavior hooks into submissive-hostile behavior. Dominant-affectionate behavior hooks into submissive-affectionate behavior. I should point out, however, that these are only probability statements. The usual pattern will be altered if one or the other decides to break off relations or not play the push-pull game. The pattern is diagrammed in Figure 5.

Dominance

Hostile-Dominance

Hostility

Hostile-Submissiveness

Submissiveness

Figure 5

Affectionate-Dominance

Affection

Affectionate Submissiveness

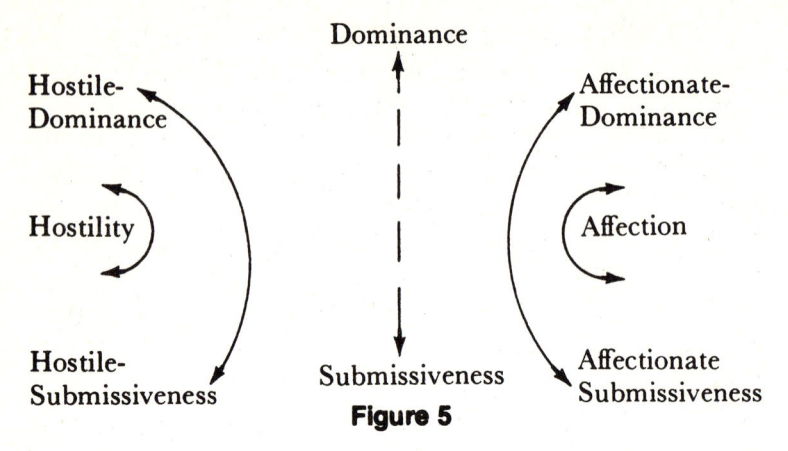

In his studies on personality Leary refined this four-quadrant system. He breaks all personality down into eight types as shown in Figure 6.

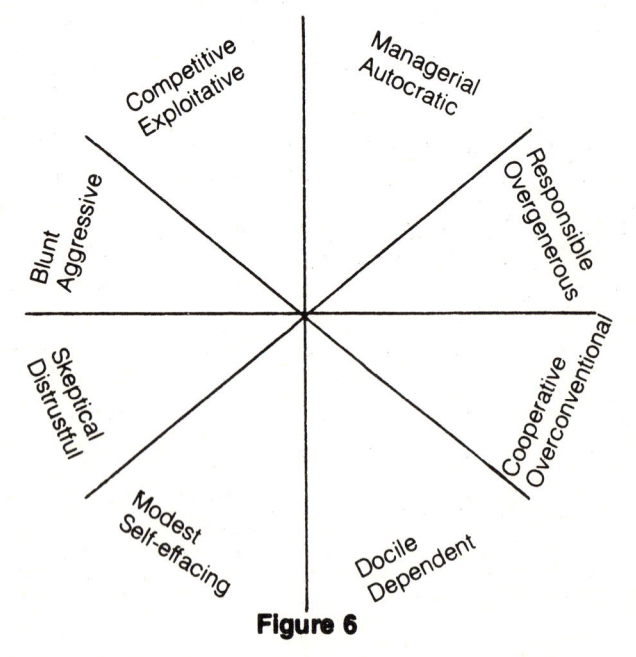

Competitive Exploitative

Managerial Autocratic

Blunt Aggressive

Responsible Overgenerous

Skeptical Distrustful

Cooperative Overconventional

Modest Self-effacing

Docile Dependent

Figure 6

Getting a Handle on Your Personality 37

The reason why he uses two words to describe each personality is that there is a balanced and an unbalanced form of each personality. In its balanced form each personality does not exhibit extreme, compulsive behavior; it is a spiritual asset. In its unbalanced expression it is extreme and compulsive; because it is unbalanced, it alienates and is a spiritual liability. Instead of using the words *balanced* and *unbalanced*, I shall use the words *adaptive* and *maladaptive*.

Now when we superimpose the eight-personality diagram on the four-quadrant diagram we have a scheme that appears in Figure 7.

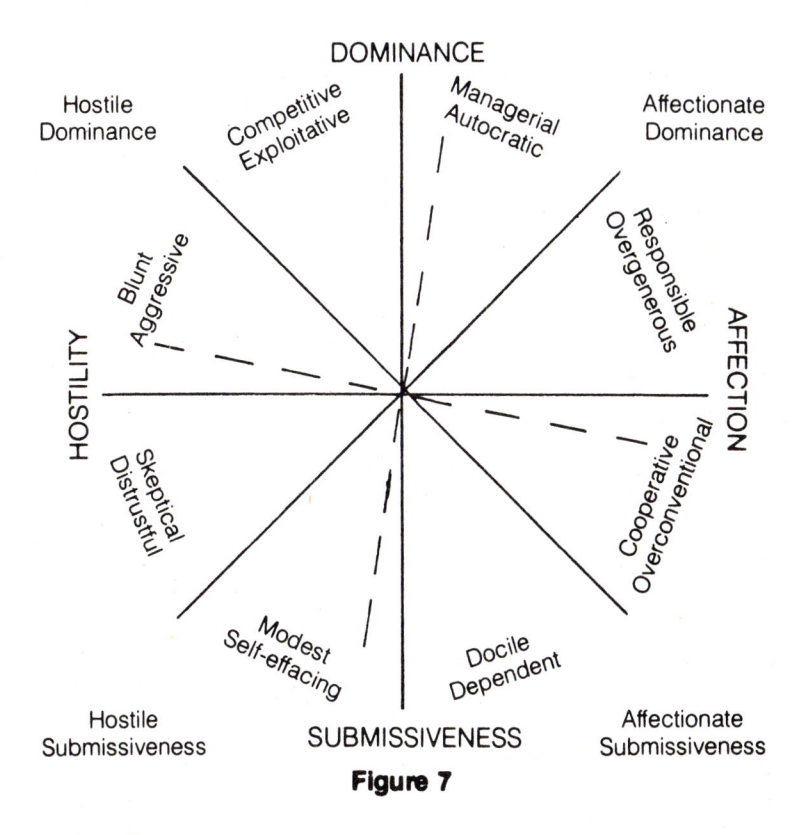

Figure 7

It will be noted that the personalities do not divide neatly along the dominant/submissive and hostile/affectionate lines. But certain generalizations may be made about each personality:

THE MANAGERIAL–AUTOCRATIC PERSONALITY
   Dominant (and either hostile or affectionate)
THE COMPETITIVE–EXPLOITIVE PERSONALITY
   Dominant and Hostile
THE BLUNT–AGGRESSIVE PERSONALITY
   Hostile (and either dominant or submissive)
THE SKEPTICAL–DISTRUSTFUL PERSONALITY
   Submissive and Hostile
THE MODEST–SELF–EFFACING PERSONALITY
   Submissive (and either hostile or affectionate)
THE DOCILE–DEPENDENT PERSONALITY
   Submissive and Affectionate
THE COOPERATIVE–OVERCONVENTIONAL
   PERSONALITY
   Affectionate (and either dominant or submissive)
THE RESPONSIBLE–HYPERNORMAL PERSONALITY
   Dominant and Affectionate

It is important that we know our personality type because it helps us to understand why we are inclined to behave as we do. We are able to discover the unique way in which we deal with the anxiety that arises in our dealings with others. But as I have stated, there are adaptive (balanced) and maladaptive (unbalanced) ways of handling our anxieties that arise from interpersonal relations.

Let us proceed to a further examination of each personality type.

Two words are used to describe each personality type. The first word describes its adaptive expression, and the second word its maladaptive expression. Think of *adaptive* and *maladaptive* in terms of degree of expression. The maladaptive is the more extreme and unbalanced form of the personality.

ADAPTIVE	MALADAPTIVE
Managerial	Autocratic
Competitive	Exploitive
Blunt	Aggressive
Skeptical	Distrustful
Modest	Self-Effacing
Docile	Dependent
Cooperative	Overconventional
Responsible	Hypernormal

When the expression of personality becomes extreme — and this is true of all eight types — relations with other people are disrupted. And it is then that personality is a spiritual liability rather than an asset.

The matter of balance in personality is the reason why I like Charles Ryrie's book *Balancing the Christian Life*. He says that a wholesome spiritual life is a life of balance. This is what interpersonal studies of personality are all about — balance! It appears that Leary, a non-Christian psychologist, has discovered by observing God's laws of human nature a truth similar to what Ryrie discovered in the Bible. It is the need for balance. Talking about the need for wholesomeness in Christian living Ryrie says,

> By wholesome I mean balance. There is nothing more devastating to the practice of spiritual living than an imbalance. One of my former teachers repeatedly reminded us that an imbalance in theology was the same as doctrinal insanity. The same applies to the realm of Christian living. An unbalanced application of the doctrines related to biblical spirituality will result in an unbalanced Christian life. Too much emphasis on the mystical may obscure the practicality of spiritual living, while an overemphasis on confession could cause unhealthy introspection, while an underemphasis might tend to make one insensitive to sin. Balance is the key to a wholesome spiritual life.[1]

In counseling Christians I find that lack of spiritual balance fits into the various maladaptive expressions of their personalities. They cannot see that they are out of balance in their spiritual perspective because it fits right into a maladaptive expression of personality, which is out of balance. We will see, for example, that the hypernormal or overconventional Christian will tend to be spiritually overbearing and alienate others with "super-spiritual" behavior. The behavior comes not of the Spirit, but of the flesh. It "feels right" because the person is fulfilling the needs of a maladaptive personality.

Let us consider briefly each of the eight personalities and how they are expressed adaptively and maladaptively. Subsequent chapters will provide a fuller treatment of each personality and show how each personality can be made a spiritual asset by its striking a balance between extreme behaviors.

THE MANAGERIAL–AUTOCRATIC PERSONALITY

In Figure 7 we saw that this personality type is definitely dominant, and it may be either hostile or affectionate. The word *managerial* describes that adaptive (balanced) expression of this personality, and the word *autocratic* expresses the maladaptive (unbalanced) expression. The difference between adaptive and maladaptive is basically the degree of dominance. The managerial personality knows how to lead and give direction without overpowering others; the autocratic person overpowers others with dictatorial behavior and coercion. The dictionary defines the autocrat as "a supreme ruler of unrestricted power; an arrogant, dictatorial person."

Few people like to be pushed around, and those who put up with the autocrat are themselves out of balance. The Christian with the autocratic personality may find his personality a spiritual liability because others resent his pushing them around. And the tragedy of this behavior is that the autocrat feels that he must be this way to hold down his anxiety and promote his self-worth.

Pastors often have this personality liability. They run their

Getting a Handle on Your Personality

churches with an iron fist, and woe be to any officer or member of the congregation who bucks him! The autocrat is fearful that if he loses absolute control, everything will fall apart. So he trades what he imagines is the greater anxiety (things falling apart) for the lesser anxiety (poor relations with other people). He imagines that poor relations with others are just a price he has to pay to do his job effectively. But this is far from the truth. Whether he uses his dominance in an affectionate or a hostile way, he still alienates others because he is inappropriately dominant. Lacking submissive traits, he is out of balance.

THE COMPETITIVE–EXPLOITIVE PERSONALITY

Figure 7 shows this personality as dominant and hostile. The mild or adaptive form is competitive. It shows a degree of dominance and a certain lack of affection (rather than raw hostility). This type of person is businesslike, but he is never so businesslike that he appears inhuman. He likes to compete, but it does not seem to be an obsession with him. He knows how to lose graciously.

The extreme or maladaptive form of this personality is the exploitive (or "exploitative") form which Leary identifies as "narcissistic." The word *narcissism* comes from the Greek mythological character Narcissus, who was cursed with a love of his own image. In interpersonal terms this behavior is seen, not only in an inappropriate exhibition of personal attractiveness, but also in a subtle form, the interpersonal message being "I am a beautiful, talented all-together person, you lucky people." Unfortunately, as we shall see in the chapter on this personality, the narcissist doesn't really believe this himself; this is why he needs many people to assure him repeatedly.

I choose to use the word *exploitive* rather than *narcissistic* to describe this person, however. Whereas the narcissistic element may be missing in some of the maladaptive forms of this personality, the exploitiveness will be there. This behavior comes out of narcissistic roots. Self-interest is the drive behind exploitation.

Again, many pastors fall into the narcissistic personality type. They tend to be strong leaders, but they usually need to have things their way. The need to be right and the tendency toward self-justification are marks of the exploiter. It is easy for him to confuse good leadership with his need to be right and to win.

The Blunt–Aggressive Personality

This personality as shown in Figure 7 is definitely hostile (or at least not affectionate) and may be either dominant or submissive.

The adaptive or mild form of this personality is called "blunt." The blunt person knows how to be firm in his dealings with others when firmness is called for. But he is fair when fairness is called for. He does know how to be pleasant and agreeable, though this is not the major expression of his behavior. Because of this balance, he is not overly blunt to the point that he alienates others.

The maladaptive expression of this personality is called "aggressive." He is an angry person and can be cruel in his words and behavior. He is seldom understood by others. They silently wonder if he doesn't know that unkind, cruel behavior alienates. The fact is that he does know; but this alienation is less threatening than close, warm relations with others.

The Skeptical–Distrustful Personality

The skeptical person, as seen in Figure 7, operates out of a submissive, nonaffectionate mode of behavior. I say "nonaffectionate" rather than "hostile" because he is not overly unfriendly. In his dealings with others he tends to be skeptical. Quiet reserve in a nonaffectionate way typifies his behavior. He is often gloomy and frequently disappointed. His approach to life is one of mild pessimism. He feels that this is good insurance against disappointment. His behavior, not being extreme, he tends to get along with others. He can be expected to be rather withdrawn, however.

The maladaptive expression of this personality is distrust. He is more than just skeptical. He is stubborn and seems to rebel against everything. This personality is also called "passive-aggressive." He is aggressive in that he operates out of a hostile mode of behavior, but passive in that he is not dominant or active in his rebellion. He simply will not move. He behaves like a silent, smoldering hunk of humanity.

I have noticed that a large number of passive-aggressive people are overweight. I get the impression that this condition facilitates their method of rebellion, which is to be an immovable object.

This does not mean to say that other personality types are not overweight. It is just that obesity seems to facilitate the maladaptive expression of this personality. The interpersonal message seems to be, "I won't fight you, but you're not about to move me."

THE MODEST–SELF-EFFACING PERSONALITY

The adaptive expression of this personality is identified with the word *modest*. This person is able to criticize self and is easily led. He definitely operates out of a submissive mode, as Figure 7 shows. He may be either affectionate or nonaffectionate (usually not to an extreme either way). The mark of this personality is submissiveness.

In its maladaptive form this personality is extremely passive and spineless. This person is usually used and abused by exploitive and aggressive persons. We see here the classic tie between the sadistic (aggressive) and the masochistic (self-effacing) person. One abuses, and the other readily permits himself to be abused.

THE DOCILE–DEPENDENT PERSONALITY

This personality tends to be more affectionate than the modest–self-effacing personality, as Figure 7 shows. Yet this type is just as submissive.

The adaptive form of this personality is identified with the word *docile*. He gives the interpersonal message, "I am trusting and eager to please." This kind of person is pleasant and very nonthreatening. The managerial and the docile personalities make a good complementary team. Such a team is often seen in husband/wife (managerial-docile) relations and in pastor/congregation (managerial-docile) relations. The managerial one is the strong leader; the docile one is the submissive, affectionate follower.

The maladaptive expression of this personality is called "dependent." This person is the proverbial "clinging vine." The interpersonal message is, "What would I do without you?" For the autocrat, whose interpersonal message is, "I am king," this kind of person provides a sick relationship. The king bestows his beneficence upon his subject, the dependent personality. And the dependent personality soaks up this attention. This relationship continues until one or the other becomes sick of the imbalance.

The dependent person tends to be a "bottomless pit." No matter how much encouragement, prayer, or sage scriptural advice he is given, this personality can't seem to get enough support. He usually has a pattern of running through one friend after another, draining each one dry in the process. Every church has its share of dependent personalities who are perpetual problem children. And because the church is committed to helping people, the pastor and other responsible people (who may be either autocratic or hypernormal) are hooked into helping these people and do not know how to get unhooked without fear of looking bad or hurting the dependent one.

The Cooperative–Overconventional Personality

Cooperation marks the adaptive expression of this personality. It is definitely affectionate and may be either dominant or submissive, but mostly submissive, as Figure 7 shows. The cooperative personality gives the interpersonal message. "I am eager to get along with you." For this reason he is close to the Christian and cultural ideal. Indeed, does not the Scripture

Getting a Handle on Your Personality

say, "Agree with your adversary while he is still in the way"? And again, "A soft answer turns away wrath. . . ."

Because of the ideals involved here, it is difficult to say anything negative about the maladaptive expression of this personality — overconventional behavior. When the overconventional person is counseled by the non-Christian counselor, he will be convinced that he is being faulted for his Christian ideals rather than for the inappropriateness of extreme behavior. He will simply write off the non-Christian counselor as "spiritually unaware."

The overconventional person goes further than the cooperative person. He is not just eager to get along, but rather goes to the extreme of agreeing with everyone at all times. He does not see the inappropriateness of his agreeability. He seems to have a lack of perspective. He just cannot see behavior in others that requires rebuke. He is a source of extreme frustration to exploitive, aggressive, and distrustful people who have no trouble fault-finding.

THE RESPONSIBLE–HYPERNORMAL PERSONALITY

Responsibility is the adaptive expression of this personality type. As shown in Figure 7, he operates from a dominant-affectionate mode. His interpersonal message is one of helpfulness. Many pastors are of this personality type, and they draw a docile following. This provides a complementary relationship that usually makes for a harmonious relationship in many churches. The same pattern is seen in many Christian marriages with the husband as the dominant-affectionate one and the wife as the submissive-affectionate one.

Because responsible behavior is close to both the Christian and the cultural ideals, it is difficult to deal with when it is taken to a maladaptive extreme (hypernormal). The hypernormal person is too willing to give of himself. In a pastor/congregation relationship the hypernormal pastor can be drained dry by dependent people. In the name of "the Lord's work" such a pastor may neglect his family, never realizing that he is responding to the demands of a maladaptive personality and not the demands of the Holy Spirit.

Everett Shostrom in *Man the Manipulator* (Bantam Books) follows Leary's personality scheme, except that he makes rigid divisions that Leary does not make. I assign *Man the Manipulator* to my clients for required reading. I will, however, follow more closely Leary's scheme and his definition of personality types.

The above survey of personality types is intended to introduce the chapters that follow. Each personality is discussed in both its adaptive (balanced, and therefore successful) expression and its maladaptive (unbalanced, and therefore unsuccessful) expression. We will see that much behavior that is rationalized as being "prompted by the Spirit" and "scriptural" has nothing to do with Christianity. *Many Christians behave as they do because of the way their personalities are organized, and not necessarily out of purely "spiritual" motives.* This is especially true of the hypernormal or overconventional Christian. These behaviors are close to Christian and cultural ideals, and therefore we are prone to assume that the behaviors are prompted by the Holy Spirit. That assumption may be unwarranted, especially if the extreme nature of the behavior alienates. More than once I have had to say to hypernormal and overconventional Christian clients that they would probably behave the same way even if they were not Christians.

One other point must be stated about Leary's theory. In determining personality type and the degree of its expression, we need to consider more than our own view of ourselves — what *we* regard our personality to be. Leary's system considers, not only how a person views himself, but also how others view him. In fact, Leary's system sees interpersonal behavior occurring at five levels.

For example, a person may report himself to be quite docile, but to others he may come across as very exploitive. In administering the Interpersonal Check List (ICL) the counselor needs the input of the person being tested and others as

Getting a Handle on Your Personality

well. The ICL is a personality test based on the theory described in this book.

I say this simply to point out that in assessing your personality type you need to know how you come across to others. Certainly one of the functions of the church as a community of believers is to bring about personality balance in each other by doing just this. Galatians 6:1 says, for example,

> Brothers, if anybody is caught in the very act of doing wrong, you who are spiritual, in a spirit of gentleness, must set him right; each of you continuing to think of yourself, for you may be tempted too (Williams).

Before we consider the eight personality types, each with it's adaptive and maladaptive form, we need to look at the method that God uses to change us and at our responsibility to submit to the process. This methodology is applied to all eight personality types in turning the maladaptive personality into its more balanced and adaptive form. Let us look, then, at a modest proposal for change.

*A Modest Proposal
for Change*

Chapter 5
A Modest Proposal for Change

How DOES A Christian go about changing a maladaptive, unbalanced personality? Psychologists have observed that mild adversity is one of the most important forces in bringing about change in human behavior and personality. James Dobson in his excellent book on child rearing, *Hide or Seek*, says,

> But I would remind you at this point that the human personality grows through mild adversity, *provided it is not crushed in the process*. Contrary to what you might believe, the ideal environment for your child is not one devoid of problems and trials. I would not, even if I could, sweep aside every hurdle from the paths of my children leaving them to glide along in mirth. They deserve the right to face problems and profit from the confrontation.[1]

This is true of adults as well as children. Just because we have reached adulthood does not mean that the growing process of personality ceases. Adults also "deserve the right to face problems and profit from the confrontation." This is the story that the Bible tells again and again in its many biographies.

For our comfort we are promised that the adversity that God brings into our lives will be mild. This is borne out in the well-known promise of 1 Corinthians 10:13. It is important to remember that this promise was given in a situation in which the Corinthians were foolishly exposing themselves to the temptation of idolatry. Paul is saying that God always provides a way of escape from trials that *He* puts on us. But when we foolishly expose ourselves to temptation, we need not expect a benevolent result.

THE DIVINE METHODOLOGY

Mild adversity is the basic method that God uses to bring about change. Whenever a person seeks counsel, it is because he has been confronted with adversity he doesn't think he can handle. The Christian counselor's task is first to determine whether the trouble is due to benevolent divine trial designed for growth, or due to the client's succumbing to temptation and the hurt that arises from it. In the latter case the counselor's ability to help is limited. He may find that all he can offer is friendship whenever the client suffers the inevitable consequences of his disobedience and be there to pick up the pieces afterward.

I fear that counselors sometimes assume that they can do for their clients what God does not offer to do — make the consequences of sin easy to bear. Trials of divine origin come with the promise that they will be bearable. Succumbing to our own temptation will bring terrible pain; but then the Christian counselor can be there, after the situation has spent itself, to help the client to pull himself together and avoid a repeat of his foolishness.

The necessity of adversity is affirmed in James 1:1-16. Verse 3 talks about trials ordained of God to bring growth. Verse 13 talks about temptations designed by Satan to pull us down. God tries us with a view to our growth; Satan tempts us with a view to defeating us.

A Modest Proposal for Change

I have said all this to emphasize the importance of adversity in growth. When adversity comes, we are encouraged to welcome it as an opportunity for growth (James 1:2,3). The foundational quality that every personality needs is patience (v. 4). The word *patience* is translated from a Greek word that means "endurance"; it means literally "to remain under." Repeated trial is designed to develop our ability to face pain without running away. But God's purpose for developing endurance is not merely to teach us how to suffer; the suffering also has the purpose of *changing* us. As we repeatedly suffer for the immature and maladaptive way in which we handle problems *we are motivated to handle them differently.*

For example, the Exploitive Personality may handle his anxiety by fighting. He can expect God to put him through trials that he will fight in his typical way, but he can expect to be bloodied when he does it. God will bring repeated trials, with the result being the same each time the exploiter tries to crash through with sheer force. The exploiter's head will be bloodied.

Now, by refusing to let up on the trial, by forcing the exploiter to endure repeated bloodying, God is *forcing* him to consider alternative ways of handling the problem. Though the person typically handles anxiety and self-worth by trying to power his way through opposition, God forces him to seek relief from his suffering in a different way. For the exploiter it would be handling the trial, not by fighting, but by submitting.

When the exploiter submits, God then reinforces that behavior by giving him peace and victory over trial. This is what I think is meant in 1 Corinthians 10:13 by "a way of escape." In any trial of God's making there is an escape-hatch. That escape-hatch, in terms of human behavior, is the different response that God is trying to cultivate in the believer. If fighting only bloodies the exploiter's head, and being more submissive wins the day, you can believe that the exploiter is going to learn *by experience* the benefit of being less driving and competitive.

Usually what happens in the early stages of change is that

we drift back to old behaviors. God responds by sending trial again. Once more, escape from the trial comes through different behavior, which is rewarded, and our resolve is reinforced to handle the problem differently the next time.

Endurance has its "perfect work" in making us more mature by forcing us to adopt alternative behaviors to cope with trial. Repeated trials mean repeated bloodying; repeated bloodying means being backed to the wall and held — to endure or remain under trial; repeatedly remaining under trial means that we begin to look for alternative ways to cope with and escape from the trial. But if we avoid trial we do not permit God to *force* us to adopt alternative behavior; we remain the same and therefore immature and maladaptive.

In Romans 5 the apostle Paul follows the same line. Tribulation works patience (endurance), patience works experience, and experience, hope. As I begin to cope successfully with trial by using different behaviors, I gain the experience of new behaviors. And when that experience is positively reinforced I can have hope in time of trial *because now I have a successful way of coping*. Nothing succeeds like success! Of course I can have hope!

Dr. Maxwell Maltz supports this view in *Psycho-Cybernetics*:

> Insofar as function is concerned the brain and nervous system constitute a marvelous and complex "goal-striving mechanism," a sort of built-in automatic guidance system which works *for* you as a "success mechanism," or *against* you as a "failure mechanism," depending on how YOU the operator operate and the goals you set forth.[2]

In 1950 during the Korean War, I was in the Air Force and was shipped to Taegu, Korea. Although the area had been fairly well cleared of Communists, a rumor circulated that guerrillas in the vicinity were creeping into the camp, cutting tent ropes, and bayonetting the men as they struggled to get out. It so happened that I heard this story the night I arrived. When I was assigned a tent that night, I was nervous; I slept with my carbine.

A Modest Proposal for Change

After a few months of living under this pressure, I gained some new skills of self-defense. I began to relax and even enjoyed exploring the countryside by myself. What had changed my feelings? Endurance under difficult circumstances forced me to come up with new coping skills.

This is why mild adversity is important to growth. Divine trial will always be bearable because God wants to see us grow, not wipe us out. The adversity might not appear mild, but if it is from God we will be able to bear it. And bear it we must, because this is how we grow.

James talks about the same process when he encourages us to ask for wisdom (v. 5). Wisdom is applied knowledge. It has to do with coping with the trial. James is not specific as to how God goes about helping us cope; he simply wants to assure us that God will give us the skills with which to cope. But only on one condition — that we really want to grow. This is why James says we are not to waiver, to be unstable like the double-minded man who one minute wants to grow in the trial and in the next breath wants to escape. Do you want to grow or don't you? Are you going to accept gladly the trials that are designed to produce growth, or aren't you? This issue must be settled first. Only then will God answer your petition for wisdom to cope.

My reference to *Psycho-Cybernetics* may seem to imply that I see a natural or human element in this matter of growth potential. Indeed, the epithet *humanist* may be hurled at me! Those who are quick to label "humanistic" anything that encourages man to draw on human resources are not well schooled in the doctrine of common grace, a subject I mentioned in an earlier chapter. They would do well to read Cornelius Van Til's booklet *Common Grace* (Philadelphia: Presbyterian and Reformed Publishing Co., 1954).

In brief, he has this to say about common grace. It is "a certain positive accomplishment in history that the sinner is enabled to make by God's gifts to him" (Ps. 145:9; Luke 6:35,36; Acts 14:16,17; 1 Tim. 4:10). It "equips human life even more thoroughly against suffering and internally brings it to richer and fuller development." The history of civilization is proof that "man is the co-laborer with God." The 1924 Synod of the Christian Reformed Church, parrying attacks on the doctrine of common grace, went so far as to say that when it comes to promoting temporal welfare "the unconverted man can even excel a regenerated person. . . . Though fallen and depraved, the natural man is still a rational creature."

Sincere Christians, desiring to hold high the banner of efficacious grace, have all but ignored common grace. In their effort to present Christ only as Savior they have ignored God's design for the revelation of Himself as a gracious God.

Common grace is God's way of daily presenting Himself to men as the gracious God who wishes to go yet further with His grace as given through Jesus Christ's atoning work. Without common grace, the theological discipline of apologetics is meaningless. I never did value the study of apologetics in the seminary until I understood common grace.

G. C. Berkouwer also writes to this point in his *Man: The Image of God*. The author outlines the view of the Dutch Calvinist theologian Abraham Kuyper, who followed in Calvin's footsteps. He said,

> Kuyper, like Calvin, is enthralled by the beautiful and imposing achievements of men outside the Church. This undeniable fact, says Kuyper, puts us before the apparent dilemma of either denying all these achievements or else viewing man as after all not completely fallen. But Reformed doctrine refuses to choose either dilemma. On the one hand, this good may not and cannot be denied; and on the other hand, the completeness of corruption may not be diminished. There is only one solution: that grace is at work even in fallen man to check the destruction which is inherited in sin.
>
> This checking of corruption is central in the whole doctrine of common grace, says Kuyper, as the holding back of the immense powers which from out of and through sin exercise their influence on human life. Kuyper considered unmistakable the phenomenon of "goodness" in sinful man, more particularly in the inclination towards good things and uprightness, things

A Modest Proposal for Change

of good report, in the voice of public conscience, and in acts of philanthropy and mercy, performed by godless man (sometimes even to the shame of believers).[3]

It is against the background of total corruption that Kuyper comes to common grace, which in innumerable instances checks the deadly working of sin. The history of the human race shows that

> on the one hand the terrible *law of sin* holds sway, but on the other hand, there was also a *law of grace*, which broke the power of sin. When the image of God in Adam stood on the verge of being wholly eradicated, divine grace intervened to "save the last remnants" of the image. Thus man was protected from becoming demonic, and common grace kept the man human. This means for Kuyper not merely an external checking and limiting. . . . Common grace for Kuyper refers not to a power from outside, an external holding back of an evil which is itself unlimited in man, but rather to a power which finds a basis in *man himself*.[4]

No informed Christian would begin to think of Abraham Kuyper as a humanist. Kuyper rightly appeals to a power in man himself grounded in the fact that common grace preserves something of the image of God even in unregenerate man. Genesis 9:6 makes it clear that the image of God does exist even in the unregenerate, or else killing a man would be no more despicable than killing a beast.

Such a theological orientation makes my talking to unregenerate clients about God's grace to them a natural occurrence. Indeed, this common grace that has given them resources to cope gives me an excellent opportunity to talk about the gracious offer of eternal life.

This is the point at which I feel the methodology of some Christian psychologists is faulty. If I take their view to its logical conclusion, I cannot help an unregenerate couple solve their marital problems unless they first are saved and experience efficacious grace. Thank God he has already made them the objects of *common grace,* a fact that gives me a marvelous opportunity to witness.

Someone is sure to say, "Well then, what advantage is there in being a Christian?" (a question analogous to the one raised in Romans 3:1). Of course the primary advantage is that of life in the new earth where Jesus Christ will reign as king. But the question will be pressed, "What advantage does the Christian have in this earth right now?"

The advantage is one of degree. In addition to all the benefits given under common grace, the Christian has the benefits of efficacious grace, which include all the works of the Holy Spirit on his behalf: the regenerating and renewing works of the Spirit, the baptizing work of the Spirit, the indwelling work of the Spirit, the sealing work of the Spirit, and the filling work of the Spirit.

I must emphasize that these benefits of efficacious grace are not offered *instead of* the benefits of common grace, but rather *in addition to*. Christians are prone to pursue "the spiritual life" with such vigor that they forget they are human beings subject to the same demands to practice mental health as any other human being. Indeed, some Christians become "so heavenly minded that they are no earthly good!" It is no wonder that some non-Christian counselors and psychotherapists regard Christianity as a threat to mental health!

I believe we need to reconsider the common evangelistic appeal to "find happiness by becoming a Christian." The fact of the matter is that becoming a Christian does not guarantee happiness, even if the Christian pursues with dedication "the spiritual life." As I stated earlier, if the Christian ignores the benefits of common grace, which provide for health and happiness, he may in reality be less happy than the unbeliever who takes advantage of the benefits of common grace. I can say without qualification that one of the greatest mistakes Christians make in their pursuit of happiness is to ignore the benefits of common grace.

What I am attempting in this book is to get back to the importance of common grace. Let's *include* the benefits of common grace as a legitimate part of Christian growth. Let's accept the responsibility for doing what we must do to change our personalities and make them a spiritual asset. We cannot be whole people by ignoring the common grace portion of God's gracious program for our growth. Only when we are enjoying the full benefits of *both* common grace and efficacious grace will we be, as the church, what Israel failed to be:

> A chosen race, a royal priesthood, a holy nation, a people for God's own possession, that you may proclaim the excellencies of Him who has called you out of darkness into His marvelous light (1 Peter 2:9).

Facilitating the Divine Methodology

Counselors do not help people to cope any more than physicians heal the sick. The counselor and the physician only facilitate the divine process. Counselors are practitioners who are aware of God's method of developing coping skills and are in the business of showing the client how the divine methodology can be put to work practically.

I have attempted to demonstrate the importance of mild adversity as foundational to the process of developing coping skills. It is the task of the counselor not to bail out the client and keep him from this adversity, but rather to guide him as he struggles with it. Remember that I am talking about *mild* adversity. The counselor does have a responsibility to warn the client to protect himself from physical, emotional, and spiritual disaster resulting from satanic temptation.

How might the divine methodology be facilitated by the Christian who is interested in growing and making his personality a spiritual asset? At least three things can facilitate the process. They are directive counseling, learning contracts, and Yokefellow groups (or similar group experience).

1. *Directive Counseling.* For the Christian who feels overwhelmed by trial, a Christian counselor who is directive helps him to put things in perspective. I refer to directive counseling, not as a particular kind of therapy, but as a general orientation

as opposed to nondirective counseling. The directive counselor is greatly concerned with directing the therapeutic process, though certainly exuding the quality foundational to all good counseling — nonpossessive warmth.

Usually, when a person seeks counseling he is confused and needs help in getting his bearings. The counselor has a responsibility to assist him in the process. He needs to help the client see his difficulty in proper perspective and to help him understand what he must *do* to cope. Much of a counselor's work is education in the art of living. This is where nondirective counseling is inadequate: it often fails to provide the client adequate information in developing coping skills. Too much counseling is just talk about the problem, and nothing is done about it.

I use a number of psychological tests to help me understand what the client lacks in coping skills and how he may well be aggravating the problem by counterproductive behavior. One of the tests I have mentioned already: the Interpersonal Adjective Check List (IACL), based on the theory of personality advanced in this book.

Part of my procedure is to go over the tests with the client and point out the behaviors that are maladaptive and need to be dropped because they are aggravating the problem. I also point out the behaviors that need to be developed to enable him to cope more effectively.

As I deal with a client in a directive way, I am in position to identify the maladaptive behaviors when they occur and to encourage more adaptive ones. I tape-record my sessions (with the client's permission) in order to demonstrate what I am talking about, and I have the client listen to the tape for homework.

For example, in dealing with a couple whose marriage is failing, I am able to identify personality traits that surface in their styles of communication. The husband may be a very dominant person, always beating down his wife with words. It is extremely helpful to confront him with this; I will describe to

A Modest Proposal for Change

him what he does and says and then play it back. The directive counselor says in essence, "Let me help you see and hear what you are doing to aggravate your problem and what you must do to change and improve your marriage." I plan to add videotape to my equipment to make this procedure even more effective.

The counselor has a responsibility to confront the client with what he is doing to disrupt relations with others and a responsibility to give direction in making changes. When God brings into your life the trial of a troubled marriage or a troubled home, He is offering you an opportunity to grow, and to do that you must be confronted with your maladaptive behavior and directed into more adaptive behavior.

2. *Learning Contracts.* When a human being suffers anxiety or low self-worth, he automatically — and usually without thinking — reacts in a self-protective manner. His personality type will depend on how he reacts. If he is a dominant or "top-dog" type, he will act assertively and with either hostility or affection. If he is submissive or an "underdog" type, he will act passively and either with hostility or affection. The maladaptive personality type will behave in an extreme way. His extreme behavior is not evident to him, but is evident to those who are close to him. As they watch the consequences of maladaptive behavior and the adversity this brings, they are in an excellent position to facilitate change. This change can be facilitated through an agreement known as a "learning contract."

A learning contract is a verbal or written agreement between the person who wants to change (the contractor) and someone close to him (the monitor) to help him monitor the behaviors that he wishes to change. Several principles should be followed in making a learning contract:

    a. The contract should be made at the initiative of the person who desires to change.

    b. The contract should list the *specific* behaviors that are to be dropped and those that are to be added.

    c. The contractor agrees that he is to be told by the

monitor whenever he displays a kind of behavior that he wants to change.
  d. The monitor agrees to tell the contractor about his behavior in a nonattacking, loving way.
  e. When the contractor is told about his behavior his only response may be, "Thank you for telling me." *He may not explain, defend, or justify his behavior in any way.* The monitor is to call to the contractor's attention any explanatory or justifying responses.
  f. The contractor is to *cease* the behavior called to his attention and substitute it with the polar behavior he wishes to develop. For example, if he is always giving advice, he is to stop giving advice and is to ask instead what the other person plans to do, or simply to remain silent.
  g. The monitor agrees to reinforce positively the changed behavior. For example, if the contractor seeks advice or is silent when he would normally give advice, the monitor should comment on how pleasing this behavior is and, if at all possible, reward that new behavior.

In appendix A is a contract form. If you wish to make a learning contract with someone, reproduce the forms in appendixes A and B or order copies at 12018 Long Ridge Lane, Bowie, Maryland 20715.

Then do the following:
1. Have one or two people who are close to you take the form in Appendix B and check those behaviors that describe you. They should put an *X* by the behaviors they like, and an *O* by the behaviors they dislike.
2. Look over the form by yourself to see how you were evaluated. Then sit down with the evaluator and ask any questions you might have about the evaluation — why certain behaviors are liked and others are disliked or what specifically the evaluator had in mind. You may not verbally attack the evaluator for his evalua-

tion; you may only ask for information. You may not defend or justify your behavior.

It is my experience that the person who really wants to change responds well to this kind of agreement. The mild adversity produced by such an agreement forces him to come to terms with his behavior day by day and to seek all the resources God offers for change. In a healthy family system this process occurs naturally. The members care for each other and therefore want to be pleasing in their behavior. They feel secure with each other, so criticism is not destructive. They are open with each other, and therefore it is natural to say in a caring way what pleases and what displeases.

The person on the edge of growth will observe a regular pattern of growth. At first he will not be aware of his maladaptive behavior until he is told. Then he will be aware of it after he has done it. Then he will be aware while he is doing it. Finally he will be aware that he is about to do it and will check himself. He will get to this place if those who love him consistently reinforce the change in behavior.

3. *Yokefellow Groups.* One of the most significant developments in recent years is the group movement. Though it is true that the concept has been abused (notably by the Esalen Institute at Big Sur, California), much good has come from group interaction. Jay Adams says of the group movement,

> Now, not all groups are wrong; not all groups are involved in these abuses. Christians must develop the use of the group form properly according to biblical norms. I have tried to point out the dangers of *many* groups today, but groups *per se* are not wrong. There is an element of truth dimly reflected by many of the ideas current among the members of these groups. For instance, we must all operate in groups; we can't avoid them. You are probably involved in more than one group today. There are groups at home (the family is a group), at church (itself a group), at the youth society (a powerful group), etc.[5]

Unfortunately Adams says that it is not a group "biblical norm" to register negative feelings about people outside the group. He says we are to do this *privately;* his justification for this is Matthew 18:15-17. But if what Adams says is true, then these feelings must not be discussed with the counselor either, unless the counselor enjoys a priestly status that the members of the group do not enjoy.

In a well-led group, no facilitator will permit it to become merely a gripe session. When negative feelings arise in a group about someone outside the group, its members should encourage a private dialogue. The group can provide much encouragement to and support of the person who must do this difficult task. What is more, a successfully operating group will make such individuals accountable to honor their resolve to settle such differences. I believe Adams himself concedes this point, because he continues,

> Groups are essential for the assimilation of new converts, for study, for sharing good things, for mutual encouragement, for instruction, and for many other biblically legitimate purposes. It is fine for a group of Christian women to get together to talk about their own inadequacies as mothers and to swap ideas about how to become better mothers. But that is quite different from these same mothers getting together to talk down their husbands. Such groups as the former must be diligent always not to allow the discussion to deteriorate.[6]

I lead groups both for clients who are in counseling and for those who wish to grow personally and enrich their marriages. I call my groups "Communication Workshops." All prospective participants are given the information sheet found in appendix C.

This kind of unstructured group inevitably requires that the leader be a committed Christian who will on one hand safeguard Christian values and, on the other hand, identify intellectualizations and rationalizations that Christians tend to use as a means of avoiding an objective, critical appraisal of themselves by brothers and sisters in Christ. And in the degree to which we avoid a critical, objective appraisal, we rob the church of its power to mold our lives.

A Modest Proposal for Change

A highly successful group movement with a Christian orientation is the Yokefellow movement. The concept of the movement is described by Cecil Osborne in *The Art of Understanding Yourself*. He states that the church is a redemptive fellowship, a group designed for Christian growth.

> During the past few years more than twelve thousand persons have been involved with our Yokefellow Groups on the West Coast. Our purpose is to help people make Christianity relevant to all life's problems and to help Christians toward a deeper commitment. Using several hundred groups for our experiment, we began to discover some important facts:
>
> First, that a person can commit to God only that part of himself which he understands and accepts; second, that a person cannot pray effectively until he deals with his emotional barriers; third, that most of these barriers are largely unconscious; fourth, that Christians by and large are not any better integrated as personalities than non-Christians; fifth, that it makes no difference whether a person is a Methodist, Lutheran, Pentecostalist, Baptist, Episcopalian, theological liberal or conservative — everyone has the same spiritual and emotional needs.
>
> Group members soon lost all sense of belonging to different denominations. Almost from the start they sensed that they were working at a deeper level than that provided by nice theological distinctions. Without surrendering any of their doctrinal beliefs, they simply moved into another realm where the reality of God and love transcended minor theological differences.[7]

Quoting Elton Trueblood, founder of the Yokefellow movement, Osborne nails down the concept of a "redemptive fellowship" when he says this:

> The world needed a saving faith, and the formula was that such a faith comes by a particular kind of fellowship. Jesus was deeply concerned for the continuation of his redemptive work after the close of His earthly existence, and His chosen method was *the formation of a redemptive society*. He did not form any army, establish a headquarters, or even write a book. All He did was to

collect a few unpromising men, inspire them with the sense of His vocation and theirs, and build their lives into an intensive fellowship of affection, worship and work.

One of the truly shocking passages of the Gospel is that in which Jesus indicates that there is absolutely no substitute for the tiny redemptive society. If this fails, He suggests, all is failure; there is no other way. He told the little bedraggled fellowship that they were actually the salt of the earth and that, if the salt should fail, there would be no adequate preservation at all. He was staking all on one throw.[8]

Persons interested in starting a Yokefellow Group should write for the booklet "New Dimensions In Spiritual Growth," Yokefellows, Inc., The Yokefellow Center, 19 Park Road, Burlingame, California 94010.

No Mud Puddles in Heaven

I do not want to give the impression that I think the foregoing suggestions will be readily picked up and followed by all readers. If my readers are as diverse as my clients, many of them are sincere wives grasping at anything to bring about change in a difficult husband. And many are difficult husbands confronted with a choice between changing or separation. Let me inject here a note of reality and hope.

Scripture teaches that God *wants* the Christian to grow and to be a mature, complete person. This means that he should be dealing effectively with problems in his marriage and with people in general regularly. If he is not, he should understand that he is in trouble with the Father. This is the teaching of Hebrews 12:1-13, the familiar "chastening passage": "Those whom the Lord loves He disciplines, and He scourges every son whom He receives" (v. 6 NASB). It should be observed that this statement is made right after the command to "run with endurance the race that is set before us" (v. 1). The point is that if we don't run with endurance, we can expect to get spanked for our unwillingness to grow up into spiritual maturity (which includes emotional maturity). Any woman married to a man who refuses to grow and thereby keeps the marriage and the

A Modest Proposal for Change

family in tension can expect to see her husband chastised. This, of course, also applies to the Christian woman who is disobedient and is keeping things in tension.

What happens when a Christian keeps matters in an uproar, in either the family or the church, and will not respond to chastisement (beginning with Matthew 18:15-20)? He can expect the Father to go the next step and execute *sin unto death!*

"Sin unto death" is a doctrine taught in 1 John 5:16 and 1 Corinthians 11:30-32 and is applied to rebellious children in Ephesians 6:2-4. Sin unto death is physical death executed on the believer who repeatedly sins and does not respond to chastisement. It may be *any* sin. In the case of the Corinthians it was abuses at the Lord's Table; because of the abuses, many were sickly (chastisement) and some "slept" (a euphemism for the death of the believer). In Ephesians 6 children are warned that they had better honor and obey parents so that their days may be long on the earth. The implication is that if they are disobedient, they may not expect a long life, but may expect it to be cut short. The sons of Eli are a good illustration of this principle (1 Sam. 2:12ff.).

The point I wish to make is that *change is not optional for the Christian.* If you or your spouse refuses to change and persists in keeping family or church in an uproar or constant tension because of unwillingness to change, God will exercise the ultimate chastisement — physical death.

When one of my sons was small, we had occasion to take a walk. A heavy rain shower had left many mud puddles near the sidewalk. At first I trusted the boy to walk beside me, but when we passed a mud puddle, he took a detour and stamped his feet in it just for kicks. I grabbed his hand, reprimanded him, and proceeded to walk with him, this time holding his hand. At the very next puddle he pulled away and did it again. This time I swatted him and told him not to do it. He cried, but became belligerent and tried to pull his hand out of mine. But I made sure he wouldn't get away. At the next puddle my son tried again to pull away, and when he didn't succeed he became furious and fought me. I decided we would have to cut short our walk: the temptation of the mud puddles was too great. I spanked him, picked him up, and carried him home. I knew that if I took him home I could clean him up and keep him clean because we had no mud puddles in the house.

There are no mud puddles in heaven. God is still in the business of "taking home" unresponsive children. This is what the history of Israel teaches us and why the Corinthians were warned,

> With most of them God was not well pleased; for they were laid low in the wilderness. Now these things happened as examples for us, that we should not crave evil things as they also craved (1 Cor. 10:5,6 NASB).

As a Christian counselor I'm never frustrated. If I am dealing with an unresponsive Christian, all I need do is take off my counselor hat and put on my prophet hat and let the disobedient client know the consequences of his behavior. I will go so far as to say that I believe some marital difficulties have been solved by sin unto death.

If I understand 1 Corinthians 5 properly, the church actually has a responsibility to commit the unresponsive believer to Satan for "the destruction of the flesh," which I understand is a death sentence (1 Cor. 5:1-8). The church does not have the right to capital punishment, but it does have the right — indeed, the responsibility — to commit an unresponsive believer to Satan in order that the death penalty might be carried out. I believe that if the church instituted such a committal service, we would get the motivation for change that we need.

What happens when a Christian man or woman is married to a professing Christian who goes on in sinful behavior without any apparent intervention on God's part — the person is neither chastised nor taken home through death. How do we explain this?

The longer I am in counseling, the more suspicious I become of professions of faith, especially when externally there seems to be no sincere desire to walk in the Spirit and there

A Modest Proposal for Change

seems to be no penalty for not walking in the Spirit. In such a case I believe the possibility of apostasy should be considered.

An apostate is one who departs from a truth he once held. He claims to be a Christian, but is not really a Christian as evidenced by his lack of fruitfulness and eventual repudiation of Christianity. This person is described in Luke 8:13 as seed that falls on a rock, germinates, but having no root "falls away." The words *fall away* are a translation of the root word also translated *apostasy*.

There is a type of faith spoken of in the Bible that appears to be genuine faith in Christ, and only time proves whether or not the faith is genuine. Two notable examples of this come to mind. Acts 8:13 speaks of Simon the sorcerer who believed and was baptized. But when he attempted to buy apostolic power, he was declared by Peter to be "in the gall of bitterness and in the bondage of iniquity" (v. 23). He never really was saved, though it is said he believed and was baptized.

In John 8:31 we are told of some Jews who had believed. But then we read in verse 44 of Jesus saying to them, "You are of your father the devil."

These are the kind of people Jude warns against in his short New Testament book. They are apostates. They have fallen from the truth they held because they really were not born-again believers. This also explains how in Jude's day they had infiltrated the church: they said all the right things; who would think they were not born again?

Now, I raise the possibility of apostasy because if the spouse is apostate, the believer is not bound to the same rules of divorce and remarriage to an apostate, who is really an unbeliever, as if married to a Christian. If the apostate conveys the message by word or deed that he really isn't interested in making the marriage work, the believer is not bound to that marriage and is free to remarry. This is clear in 1 Corinthians 7; "Yet if the unbelieving one leaves [the Greek word is *divorce*], let him leave; the brother or the sister is not under bondage [to stay in the marriage as in vv. 12-14] in such cases, but God has called us to peace" (v. 15). The unbeliever might convey this message through behavior that is hurtful and destructive to the marriage, behavior that says he is unwilling to change. In such a case the believer is free to divorce and remarry. Sometimes, should a believer make a move to divorce, the apostate or professing Christian will come around to work on the marriage.

If God puts two believers into a marriage where there is virtually no justification for divorce and remarriage (as taught in Matt. 19:9), it would seem that some safeguards are built in. And I believe they are. A Christian spouse who refuses to make a marriage work can expect to be chastened, and if he does not respond to the chastening, he can expect sin unto death. If a professing Christian seems to get away with destructive behavior without chastisement or ultimately sin unto death, then we ought to raise seriously the question of apostasy.

The Managerial-
Autocratic Personality

Chapter 6
The Managerial-Autocratic Personality

WHEN I MET Lance,[1] my first impulse was to genuflect, bow, and scrape or otherwise show obeisance. His interpersonal message was clearly "I am King!" In terms of interpersonal diagnosis of personality, he was an autocrat.

THE AUTOCRATIC PERSONALITY

The Autocratic Personality is characterized by domineering behavior. He compulsively attempts to control and overorganize his life and the lives of those around him. He gives the appearance of competence and efficiency.

Lance's wife initiated counseling because she felt she could no longer live with him. "He is smothering me," she said. "Living with him is a dehumanizing experience, and my health is suffering." Her doctor concurred: she was suffering from a severe case of colitis.

Lance justified his behavior on the ground that Ephesians 5 declares the husband is the head of the wife. Anything good the Bible had to say about power or conquest he seized upon. In fact, the Book of Joshua was his favorite book of the Bible. "The land of Canaan wasn't conquered by a bunch of pantywaists": this statement was made repeatedly to those who called attention to his excessive use of force.

Whenever Lance's wife balked at his power plays and domination, he would counter with stern warnings that she was not being a submissive wife. And the word *submissive* took effect every time.

"It's not that I don't want to be submissive," Lance's wife told me. "I just want a chance to do something my way once. Isn't a woman supposed to manage the household? He makes all the decisions about what the menu will be, how we furnish the house, how I organize my kitchen, how I do the laundry." She was angry. "He's turning me into a vegetable."

As she viewed it, Lance was not only dictatorial and dominating but also lacked any submissive traits that might have tempered his dominance. He would never apologize and would not bring himself to admit that he ever was wrong.

Why did Lance behave this way? He felt most secure when he was in control. He also found an admiring following in the church, and this fact gave him great feelings of self-worth and reinforced his power-oriented behavior. Whenever he was in a situation he did not control, he would either attempt to seize control or leave the field of action with righteous indignation. His attitude was "The king will not dignify the discussion with his presence."

When the Autocratic Personality is found in a pastor, the church faces the danger of a power struggle between the pastor and others in the church who also find their security and self-worth in controlling. Such personalities tend to pull support from Docile-Dependent Personalities in the church who will flatter, respect, and obey them. Power struggles between autocratic people have divided many a church into warring camps. Too often it is not the issues that are responsible for factionalism; the real problem is with the autocratic personalities who lead the power struggle. They confuse their ego

The Managerial-Autocratic Personality

need to be right with what is objectively right for the particular congregation. The apostle John had trouble with such a person named Diotrephes, who, according to John, "loveth to have the preeminence among them" (3 John 9).

The autocratic pastor also faces the danger of being hooked into a sick relationship with dependent people in his church, especially dependent women. Frequently the woman with a dependent personality will find a great deal of security and self-worth in the attention given to her by the autocratic pastor. He gets what he wants — flattery and obedience; she gets what she wants — someone to watch over her and protect her. Doctors and other professional men tend to have the same problem.

The seeds of sexual involvement are often planted in this kind of relationship, and the thing that makes it dangerous for the pastor is that the initial appeal is not sex. It is the satisfaction of a basic psychological need — the need to hold down anxiety and to feel self-worth. *She* doesn't buck him or fight him as his wife does. *She* knows how to be a submissive woman. His wife may not flatter, respect, or obey him, but *she* does. It's nice to be around her because she is feeding his ego. And when they discover that it feels good to be near each other, it's only a short step to sexual involvement.

People in Christian vocations or considering one must be very careful not to confuse what feels good and right to them with what is commonly referred to as "the call of God." The pastorate and certain other Christian vocations offer the Christian an excellent opportunity to indulge his compulsive dominance over others.

What a dangerous combination — an autocrat who feels that he has "the call of God!" What authority he feels he has as God's spokesman! How dare anyone stand in the way of God's servant!

This type of person will often wear a facade of false humility. In fact, when the IACL is administered, he may report only mild dominance whereas others report extreme dominance.

Tragically this person finds it difficult to see the inappropriateness of his behavior or see the condescending way he treats others.

Autocratic behavior is compulsive. There is an inner drive that operates beyond reason. The compulsive autocrat is one who is active, prompt, well-organized, industrious, pedantic, planful, and often righteously competent. He is clearly trying to impress others with his effectiveness. But the very compulsive nature of his behavior is a symptom of guilt or impotency. If he really believed he were as capable as he pretended to be, he wouldn't work so hard to prove it!

It must be remembered that I am not describing unregenerate people only. This personality type is common to the regenerate as well. Church history offers many examples, one of the most colorful being that of Martin Stephan, the Bohemian preacher who led a group of Germans to the backwoods of Missouri in the late fall of 1838. Carl Mundinger, in his book *Government in the Missouri Synod*, says that Stephan was a man of unusually powerful persuasion.

> Men of learning and men of ignorance, men of wealth and men of poverty, were hypnotized by the spell of his spoken word and were persuaded to part with things most dear to their hearts....
>
> To some of his contemporaries [Stephan] was a saint, to others Satan incarnate, to still others a psychological riddle.
>
> Psychology may help us to understand him. Whatever attitude one may take toward the "guilt" or "innocence" of Martin Stephan, this much is certain — his was a maladjusted personality.[2]

Mundinger goes on to tell the story of how Stephan gained incredible control over his congregation. Imagining himself to be God's prophet, Stephan in reality was victimized by an Autocratic Personality. When it came to democratic government in the church, Stephan could not stand a negative vote; he maintained such control over his people that they would rubber-stamp everything. Mundinger observes,

> A dictator wants a *"Ja"* vote. A man who cannot vote *"Ja"* is a traitor, or, as Stephan would say, he is not true. . . .
>
> Let us remember that he was a pastor in Saxony, where pastors were surrounded with a certain halo. They were *Standespersonen*. As a member of a privileged class, his word carried weight.[3]

Mundinger points out that Stephan's autocratic behavior was really a facade to cover feelings of inferiority. He compensated for this by gaining complete control over others. The pastorate offered him an excellent opportunity to do so in a socially acceptable way — at least so Stephan thought. At any rate, it is clear that Stephan confused his "divine mission" with a maladjusted personality that attempted to control others as a means of giving him feelings of worth.

Stephan's dedication to his work is reminiscent of what I see in some pastors still today:

> Stephan's tremendous zeal in the discharge of the duties of his office led him to forget the social needs of his family — this combination of circumstances and events was bound to have its effects in the disorganization of Stephan's personality.[4]

The disintegration of his marriage led Stephan to seek female companionship elsewhere. This was, in addition to his dictatorial ways, one of the final things that led to his downfall. Stephan the *Standespersonen* even fancied himself to be above the morality of the common man!

Mundinger, summing up the personality of Martin Stephan, says this:

> Martin Stephan, then, was a definitely maladjusted person. . . . His maladjustments were exaggerated by domestic discord, which had its origin in cultural and sexual differentiations. He compensated for his feeling of inferiority by persecutory delusions and by getting absolute control over certain human beings and by social intimacy with his male and female adherents.[5]

The spirit of Stephan still lives in many churches. And it is a difficult one to exorcise. I speak of the spirit not only as found in pastors, but also in laymen. In the case of Lance his maladaptive Autocratic Personality was a definite spiritual liability. In the name of being a leader in the church and of being his wife's head and savior, he was destroying relations with people in the church and with his wife and children. He could understand the organizational relationship of the husband and wife where the husband is the head of the wife, but he chose to ignore the in-grace-relationship of 1 Peter 3:7, where the wife is said to be co-heir with the husband. Whenever this was called to his attention, his response was, "Yes, but. . . ."

The task I had before me with Lance was to reduce the intensity of his dominance by purging some of the extreme dominant behaviors and adding some submissive ones. I sought to strike a balance between dominance and submissiveness. He needed to see that sometimes it was all right to be dominant, but at other times he needed to give in. I did not attempt to change his personality type, but rather attempted to make it more adaptive as reflected in the Managerial Personality.

THE MANAGERIAL PERSONALITY

The Managerial Personality is less dominant than the Autocratic Personality, though he is still a good leader and likes responsibility. He has an aura of competence, strength, and authority about him, but he could never be called dictatorial. He does not have to control everything and can move into a new social or business situation without compulsively taking over.

My task for Lance was first to get him to drop some of his maladaptive dominant behavior. He was always giving advice, even though he didn't realize it. He needed to be told whenever he did this. He also was encouraged to let others take the lead and to admit it when he was wrong.

In moving Lance's personality to its more adaptive form I made a list of the actions he was to drop and those he was to add to his repertoire of behavior. He was to drop the following:

The Managerial-Autocratic Personality

>Domination of others
>Acting impressed with his importance
>Planning the lives of other people for them
>Acting dictatorial
>Insisting his way is the best
>Expecting others to obey and admire him
>Always engaging in some activity showing off his physical or intellectual strength
>Justifying his behavior
>Being excessively planful

The following submissive behaviors were to be added:

>Admit it when wrong on important matters
>Apologize when he wronged someone
>Follow the directions of others
>Let others do things for him
>Sit quietly and let others talk
>Occasionally do things spontaneously and without plan
>Occasionally sit and do nothing

To facilitate these objectives I spurred Lance to make learning contracts with his wife. I also dealt with him in private and group counseling. The group, constituted of Christians, was designed to bring social pressure to bear on Lance's dominance. Lance's first jolt came in the group: whenever he began to take over or insist on his being right, they would shoot him down. The group is handled in an unstructured way, the leader permitting the group to establish its own direction. This provided a marvelous opportunity for Lance to take over. After a few minutes of awkward silence in the first session, Lance said, "Well, it appears that we ought to get organized and establish some goals if the leader isn't going to give us any."

With that he proceeded to lecture the group on what he thought ought to be done. When he was finished, one of the braver members of the group asked Lance, "Who made you the group leader?"

With typical justification Lance shot back, and the group was off to a good start. Before the evening was over, every member of the group was sharing with Lance his or her resentment over his coming in and taking over. In the following weeks Lance was made painfully aware of what he was doing to alienate others; his wife was not the only one who felt the way she did about him. The response of the group also provided an opportunity to recondition Lance's behavior. Rather than be rewarded for taking over, he was rebuffed. And when he was praised for not taking over and letting others take the lead, he began to realize that he could handle his anxiety and problems of self-worth much better by being less dominant. Group pressure in a Christian context can be an effective aid in turning a personality that is a spiritual liability into a spiritual asset.

This is why it is important to grasp the concept of James 1 — the primacy of trial in changing the life of the Christian. Trials come through contact with other people, believers and nonbelievers alike.

Another method employed in reducing Lance's dominant behavior was the "learning contract." Lance agreed he wanted to know whenever he came across to his wife in a dominant way. The verbal contract stated that whenever Lance's wife began to feel he was too free with his advice, she was to tell him that she was annoyed with it. Lance could only respond "Thank you for telling me" and then stop dispensing advice on the matter at hand. This stipulation forbade his justifying, rationalizing, or defending his behavior. The only thing he needed to know was when his behavior was offensive, so he could stop it.

Besides private counseling, learning contracts, and groups, I had given Lance the Interpersonal Adjective Check List (IACL) to identify the specific behaviors that needed to be changed and to show the extreme degree to which he was committed to his behavior. I also arranged for his wife and teenage children to give him the test. Objective testing enables both the counselor and client to talk about specific behaviors and keeps them from getting lost in generalities.

The Managerial-Autocratic Personality

In directive counseling I pointed out to Lance that he had to reduce his dominance. I provided a copy of Publication 510 from the American Institute of Family Relations (AIFR). The title: "Suggestions for Decreasing Dominance." The publication suggests that dominating behavior can be reduced by observing the following:

1. Recognize that you do get unreasonably angry at times, and find several satisfying and effective ways to use or deflect the energy of your anger.
2. Learn to recognize exactly what the obstacle is that is frustrating you.
3. Find out if the obstacle you see is *really* an obstacle, or if it seems to be one only because you see it that way. Are you fighting real dragons or only windmills?
4. When you know what the obstacle is, and you are sure it is actually an obstacle, then find the best way to deal with it effectively.[6]

Each of these suggestions is followed with a number of particulars that give direction in implementing them.

The Competitive-Exploitive Personality

Chapter 7
The Competitive-Exploitive Personality

THE COMPETITIVE-EXPLOITIVE Personality is not inclined to seek counsel. This is mainly because competitive people feel most threatened when they show weakness or dependence.

THE EXPLOITIVE PERSONALITY

This personality type in its exploitive extreme is sometimes identified as narcissistic. He expresses a clear love and approval of himself. He behaves in a strong, arrogant manner and communicates to others that he feels superior. He acts independent and confident, though secretly his confidence is a facade to cover real feelings of inadequacy.

I remember discovering in my early teens that if I appeared confident and sure of myself, I could walk into almost any situation unchallenged. I enjoyed getting dressed up and walking into some of New York City's finest hotels and salons as though I belonged. If challenged by a doorman's questioning look, I would return it with disdain and walk right past him. If verbally challenged, I could really put him down with a "Who do you think you are?" response. The name of the game was to appear self-confident and to intimidate and defeat any challenger.

The self-confident narcissist may exhibit his personality in a number of ways. He may flex his muscles, give much attention to dress and grooming, or flaunt his wisdom, which he tells himself is far superior to that of those he regards as inferior. In the extreme this person seems driven to boost himself compulsively at the expense of others. He often will be extremely jealous over the success of others. He is driven to compete, exhibit, and exploit. He is rejective and selfish, though this selfishness may be covered by the appearance of doing good for others.

This personality often seeks vocations that involve public display, such as modeling, acting, and even the pastoral ministry. Though God may use and even sanctify a man's love of being before people, such a man must be careful to recognize the dangers of this personality in its extreme.

When I read in Genesis the story of Joseph the son of Jacob, I get the impression that seventeen-year-old Joseph was a self-confident narcissist. God used thirteen years of suffering and adversity to temper this young man and to make him more emotionally and spiritually balanced for the success that was to follow.

This personality, when found in the Christian, can be detrimental to conscious spiritual goals. His coldness and indifference carries the interpersonal message, "I don't care about you." In the church this can be disruptive to good relations that require a caring spirit. It is usually not recognized that this attitude is a defensive maneuver. If the exploiter cared, he could not push for his own goals ruthlessly; the ability not to care facilitates his ruthlessness.

The exploiter maintains that he is right about almost everything. On minor issues he may concede a point, but this is to lay to rest the criticism that he always has to be right.

Even in games he can be ruthless about winning. The

The Competitive-Exploitive Personality

exploiter, fearing damage to his self-confident narcissism, feels he must win to preserve his status. The compulsive, frantic attempts of the exploiter to win often produce inappropriate behavior that is evident to everyone but himself.

The exploiter, bent on his self-confident narcissism, is really not interested in pleasing others. He is interested only in pleasing himself with activities that are self-enhancing. Such maneuvers can be subtle, however: he may give freely of his time, money, and energies to others — not really for their sake, but for his self-enhancement. He manipulates others into admiring him as a strong benefactor. He is bent on triumphing over others and defeating them.

This personality is a spiritual liability in that it lacks the balance of some of the more submissive and loving traits the Bible commends. I recall what this lack of balance did to my understanding of 2 Timothy 4:2: This was one of my favorite portions of Scripture as a preacher. What a mandate to indulge my self-confident narcissism! "Reprove!" said the apostle. "Rebuke!" said the apostle. "Exhort!" said the apostle. Ah, I was good at that — but wait! He continues. He says it is to be done "with all patience and instruction" (NASB). Here is the balance. Preachers are not to be sadistic mutilators, but surgeons of the soul who can cut with compassion.

It may be asked why a person would behave in such a cold, unfeeling way. The answer is that they are not always aware of their behavior. But they certainly are aware of their feelings. They are feeling anxious and have low self-worth. They cannot bear the anxiety of weakness or dependence so they appear strong, self-confident, assertive, and independent. The facade is designed to fool anyone who might take advantage of what they imagine to be weakness in themselves. And the more anxiety-ridden this person is, the more he steps up his security operation of independence and attempted triumph over others. He looks for opportunities to compete and win.

It may seem that the obvious solution is to reason with this person from Scripture, but the problem is that he does not see the inappropriateness of his behavior. He will argue that his behavior is right. He will reply, "Doesn't the Bible say to reprove, rebuke, and exhort? Yes, we are to do it with long-suffering, but you would water down the power of the Word with the emphasis you place on long-suffering!" He doesn't realize that he deemphasizes long-suffering, because deep down he is very insecure about appearing soft. In fact, the accomplished exploiter may have buried his feelings of inadequacy so deeply that he does not even know they are there. Here is where counseling can help this person get in touch with feelings of inadequacy — if he will bear taking a dependent posture for once in his life. Injury to his narcissism is the most frequent reason this personality seeks counsel. And God is still in the business of injuring narcissism, just as He did in Joseph, to bring the self-confident narcissist to task.

It should be said about the exploiter that his personality is most vulnerable to the interpersonal push-pull of the Modest–Self-Effacing Personality. The exploiter offers strength (in a nonaffectionate way). And the self-effacing person needs that strength, but because of poor self-image he really doesn't expect to be loved. The self-effacer who gets involved with the exploiter is in for much pain because he is being used to enhance the power of the exploiter.

In one case a self-effacing woman locked into a relationship with an exploiting male was used so many times that she attempted suicide. She finally saw that she was being used, and her anger at the exploiter produced a resolve to live. She would not feed his narcissism by killing herself over him. What is more, she dealt his narcissism a severe blow by breaking off with him.

Sometimes the exploiter is a nagging wife, and the self-effacing person is an alcoholic husband. Some women find that such a relationship feeds their feelings of female superiority and their hatred for males ("Look at the drunken bum!"). She, of course, provides him a service too: she reinforces his view of himself — that he is a no-good bum. This gives him an excuse to

The Competitive-Exploitive Personality

drink. No-good bums are supposed to drink. "What is more," his reasoning goes, "if you had a wife like mine, you'd drink too."

Writing in *Christianity Today* magazine, I attempted to alert pastors to another dangerous form of this push-pull in an article entitled "The Pastor and the Other Woman." Writing about the narcissist, I point out that

> the narcissist holds down anxiety and promotes a feeling of self-worth by impressing others with his competence and attractiveness. He does this by muscle flexing, boasting, and engaging in seductive and flirtatious maneuvers. He "pushes" the message "I'm wonderful," and this behavior "pulls" dependence and admiration from others. The narcissist enjoys compliments on his attractiveness from men, women, and even children. And because of this he will disclaim particular gratification over compliments from women. Nevertheless, he is particularly pleased at being noticed by women.
>
> In the church this interpersonal "push-pull" can be dynamite. Here is a man who needs to be told he is strong, competent, and attractive. In his congregation there are likely to be one or more women who feel dependent. Such women often feel unloved, and they may have weak, unattractive husbands. They find in such a pastor their ideal of a man. And because he is a *spiritual* man he is even more attractive. It does not take much verbal or nonverbal exchange for two people like this to become locked into a very fulfilling complementary relationship. He receives from her admiration and dependence, and she receives from him loving, protective care through his pastoral ministry — which can easily degenerate into a very personal and intimate interest.
>
> Meanwhile, back at the parsonage, the pastor's wife is troubled over her husband's response to the admiring women of the congregation. She wonders about his feelings for her. If he were satisfied with her, why should he bask in the attention of other women? Resentment, distrust, and withdrawal follow. He gets the nonverbal message from his wife, "I don't think you're so great," which makes him all the more vulnerable to the admiring words and looks of the women in his congregation.

> The tragedy of the compulsive narcissist is that his security operation is designed to cover up real feelings of inadequacy. Rather than face these tormenting feelings and deal with them, he uses his narcissistic facade to pull from people the message that he is not as inadequate as he feels. . . .
>
> Why does the narcissist prefer the admiration of women other than his wife when, after all, she was once his greatest admirer? The answer lies in the nature of maladaptive narcissism. The maladaptive narcissist is so hungry for admiration that one woman's is not enough. He needs many admirers to keep his faltering ego built up.
>
> It is my contention that the minister who errs sexually does not start out with sexual encounter on his mind. He starts out to build his ego on the admiration of all the people in his congregation — men, women and children. The women of the congregation provide ego satisfaction for his doubts about his masculinity. These doubts are allayed by messages from the women that he is an attractive male. He then finds himself with the opportunity to check out these messages more fully.
>
> The wiles of the devil are extremely subtle. Every man starts his ministry knowing full well the dangers of involvement with women in the church. It is through a circuitous route that Satan traps the man. The trap is deadly because the bait is not sex. The bait is ego satisfaction, a normal human need; *this leads* to an opportunity for sexual involvement.[1]

Caution for the clergy is also raised by the well-known newspaper columnist, Ann Landers, who conducted a sort of "lechery poll." According to a recent *New York Times Sunday Magazine* article, in a profile that she compiled at a reader's request, a survey was made among women to determine which male — by occupation — most frequently tried to seduce them. Said the article,

> At final count, it was doctors by a stethoscope; clergy collared second, with dentists catching up, lawyers gaining and professors — "it's that or flunk" — closing fast.

THE COMPETITIVE PERSONALITY

If the Exploitive Personality is to move to its more adap-

The Competitive-Exploitive Personality

tive form, the Competitive Personality, the following behaviors must be dropped:

> Exhibitionism and self-enhancement
> Always talking about self and building self up
> Defensiveness and all attempts to explain and justify self
> Intense concern over dress and grooming
> Superior attitudes
> Independent to the degree he feels he needs no one
> Ruthlessness in dealing with others
> Always needing to win in competition
> Seductiveness and flirtatiousness
> Compulsively seeking success
> Self-righteousness

The following submissive-affectionate traits should be added to give balance:

> Grateful
> Admires and imitates others
> Appreciative
> Eager to be approved of
> Often helped by others
> Very respective of authority
> Accepts advice readily
> Trusting and eager to please

The great fear of the exploiter who engages in self-confident narcissism is that any tempering of his behavior will lead to defeat. He reasons that if he is barely succeeding by fighting every battle tooth and nail, he certainly will not make it at all if he behaves more submissively and affectionately.

In reality the opposite is true. The man who is less compulsive and relaxed about his work has far more energy to spend in getting the job done. The exploiter tends to spend too much energy planning, preparing, and executing. All that energy is not spent because his work demands it; it is spent because he is afraid of failure!

When I read of General Bull Moose, corporation executive, working fifteen hours a day, I am a bit skeptical about promoting this as an ideal to be strived for. The executive may object, "But the job demands it!" That is fine — if the job demands it. Too often it is not the job, but the exploiter's fear of failure that drives him so.

The *Reader's Digest* ran an article on this personality, called "Your Personality May Be Killing You." This article identified two personality types: Type A, the driving heart-attack-prone type, and Type B, the more relaxed and less susceptible to heart attack. The article said,

> The two characteristics of Type A behavior are "hurry sickness" and "free floating hostility...." Such individuals are in what [researchers] call a "chronic continuous struggle." If the struggle is not abated, they suspect, it will do little good to alter one's diet, smoking or exercise habit. Behavior patterns are more a state of mind than station in life....
>
> Type B people, by definition, have personalities that are the opposite of Type As. This doesn't mean Type B people are incapable of hard work, achievement, and advancing to lofty positions. In fact, they generally make better executives because they don't rush decisions, make snap judgments, or antagonize their subordinates.[2]

The article observes further that the B type knows his capabilities and limitations, but the A type doesn't, and doesn't wish to.

I recall coming to terms with this in my own life. How I wept in frustration and fear when I faced the prospect of having to slow down. Maybe I would fail! This was a fate worse than death. If I died, at least I wouldn't have to face my friends with the humiliation of failure. Those who live with the exploiter need to appreciate this terrible fear.

My experience in moving to a more adaptive form of this personality, the Competitive Personality, is that I have far more energy to do my work than I ever had before. I am not spending all that energy now fighting fear of failure and nursing

The Competitive-Exploitive Personality

my narcissism. At one time I suffered excruciating chest pains from hypertension. I have been free of this for five years now. I have not yet arrived, and I won't until I see Jesus and am made like Him. But I do feel liberated from the fear of failure. I can honestly say that failures have become valuable teachers.

The value of this personality change in improving the spiritual life is immeasurable. One of the benefits is the ability to cope with jealousy. The exploiter can't stand success in others, because it puts someone else in the spotlight. But when he doesn't have that craving for the spotlight, he is not jealous when it is focused on others — or at least when he is jealous, he knows that his narcissism is acting up.

Such a relaxed approach to work can be a benefit to the family. The exploiter often feels in a bind between "the demands of work" and the need of his family. Often the family feels neglected and bitter because they see the exploiter giving the job energy that seems unnecessary. The exploiter who wishes to become more adaptive in his personality type — the competitor — will want to adopt the same suggestions outlined in the chapter "A Modest Proposal for Change": directive counseling, learning contracts, and groups — Yokefellow or other groups whose objectives are consistent with the Bible.

In directive counseling the counselor will often find the client wrestling for control of the session. It is important that the counselor not come across as a threat to the competitive client; he must exhibit nonpossessive warmth. On the other hand, the counselor must be careful that he does not permit the client to control the session. Competition with the counselor must be handled with empathy, warmth, and genuineness, but it must be dealt with.

When learning contracts are used, the monitor may expect that this personality will attempt to explain or justify his position. It is important, when making a contract (as found in appendix A), that the following provisions be emphasized:

> The contractor can only reply "Thank you for telling me" when the monitor fulfills the terms of the contract, and he

cannot explain, defend, or justify his behavior. The monitor is to call it to his attention whenever he defends or justifies himself.

This may be difficult for the monitor to do, especially if she is the contractor's wife, and she is a Self-Effacing or Dependent Personality. But this will present her with the opportunity to be a more assertive person, something that will help her become a balanced person.

As for group exposure, I believe this personality receives the greatest impact on his behavior from the group simply because he finds it difficult to justify his behavior when many of his peers are all saying the same thing. Groups may be a personal bias on my part, however, because I found a group experience most effective in changing me, as I have related in the first chapter, "Lord, Cut Me Gently."

The Blunt-Aggressive Personality

Chapter 8
The Blunt-Aggressive Personality

THE BLUNT-AGGRESSIVE Personality is a fascinating study, especially when seen in its maladaptive expression of aggression. Why should a person select negative, hostile expressions as a means of security, especially Christians whose ideals would seem to mitigate against such behavior?

THE AGGRESSIVE PERSONALITY

As we have seen already, every personality has both an adaptive (balanced) and a maladaptive (unbalanced) expression. The maladaptive expression of this personality type is the aggressive person. He seems to delight in combat, feels comfortable only when engaged in a threatening attack, experiences no qualms at punishing others and appears to feel weakened and threatened by the prospect of collaborative, tender, or docile impulses.

Several years ago I was vacationing with my family at a well-known Bible conference. The director and his wife were nationally known for their abrasiveness. My sister was talking to the director's wife one day about one of the current battles the organization was engaged in, and during the conversation the director's wife said with great relish, "There's nothing I like better than a good fight!"

This woman was highly respected for her "Christian testimony" and "convictions," but as I thought about this encounter I came to realize that more than "convictions" were involved in her response to people. There was something compulsive about her aggressiveness that defied the reason of reasonable men.

Strangely enough, most individuals who fall into this category are in the ranks of the socially approved. The military, law enforcement agencies, and penal institutions often attract this personality. His job presents an opportunity to do what he is most comfortable with — to administer insult, derogation, or punishment. In fairness to the above-mentioned institutions, I add that pains are usually taken to screen out the extremely aggressive person, but people with this personality are indeed most comfortable in such work.

This personality does not go around beating up those who stand in his way. Rather, his aggressiveness is expressed in his attitude, which is disciplinary, sarcastic, and guilt-provoking. His stern toughness is often admired and supported by those who serve with him in jobs and activities that may well require sternness. When this person brings his attitude home from work with him, then the trouble starts. It may be the critical, hostile, unforgiving army colonel who comes home from a day at the Pentagon and attempts to run his family like a military organization. It may be the sharp-tongued, bad-tempered, mocking head nurse who carries her behavior over into her social life and thereby destroys interpersonal relations with those in her social circle.

This behavior is seen most clearly in New Testament Pharisaism and is carried over into the church today in various forms if "righteous indignation." I do not mean to say that righteous indignation is improper. When it comes from loving, long-suffering, compassionate believers it is believable, because

The Blunt-Aggressive Personality

they show a balance between affection and hostility. But when it comes from the punishing, stern, unforgiving Aggressive Personality, righteous indignation, so-called, simply becomes an excuse, a rationalization, to engage in the favorite pastime of lashing out at others. The Bible again and again is used by this personality as an excuse to do what he is disposed to do.

What is the purpose of aggressive behavior? Why does a person engage in that which obviously alienates? The hostile, punitive person feels that this behavior is most effective in minimizing anxiety. He does not decide at the conscious level to behave this way, but acts more out of an unconscious reflex. These reflexes convey to others the message of toughness. He intends to convey the message, "Don't fool with me; you'll get hurt if you try." Though tender, agreeable, and warm feelings may be cited as Christian virtues, this personality will argue that they would be inappropriate for him. The truth is that he feels threatened by anything that would take away from his hard-boiled defenses.

One of the interesting features of this personality, especially when operating in the church, is his sense of righteousness and piousness. He feels perfectly justified in taking a stern, tough, hard-boiled posture. His hurtful, mocking, sarcastic behavior is a form of moral coercion. He sees nothing wrong with this behavior, because he is "simply trying to straighten people out."

Such persons often fill authoritative positions in the church. The church as an organization may actually provide him opportunity to engage in pious, righteous discipline and moral coercion.

The Reverend Hale in James A. Michener's novel *Hawaii* is a good example. He was all too ready to throw down the heathen shrines and condemn the practices of the heathen. His position as a missionary gave him ample opportunity to display his aggressiveness, of course, "in the name of God." How the name of God and the cause of Christ are used and abused by this personality!

It is difficult to combat the moves of such people. Their cause may be good. They may be bent on eradicating some evil in the church or community. But intuitively — and I hope by sensitivity to the Holy Spirit — the well-adjusted believer senses something is wrong about the manner in which the crusader goes about his work. The Aggressive Personality's devotion to "duty" seems to go beyond the calling of God into a personal struggle. Those who dare say anything negative about the crusade are themselves in danger of being mocked, humiliated, and being branded as "agents of Satan."

The Aggressive Personality, like any other personality, is engaged in a struggle to reduce anxiety and promote self-worth. This person reduces his anxiety by establishing distance from the feared person or object. He does this in a more dominant way than the Skeptical-Distrustful Personality, who is more passive and sneaky in the way he creates distance. The Aggressive Personality is afraid that if he becomes more yielding and loving, others may gain the advantage over him. He believes he needs to convey the message that he is not a pushover.

Everett L. Shostrom calls this personality "The Judge." He says,

> The Judge exaggerates his criticalness. He distrusts everybody and is blameful, resentful, slow to forgive. Variations of the Judge are the Know-It-All, the Blamer, the Deacon, the Resentment Collector, the Shoulder, the Shamer, the Comparer, the Vindicator, the Convictor.[1]

As I write this chapter, the *Washington* (D.C.) *Star* newspaper reports on such a person — Superior Court Judge Edward A. Beard. The newspaper story says,

> Telling people things "in no uncertain way" is Beard's specialty, and he has been called down for it numerous times by the normally restrained D.C. Court of Appeals.
>
> "We view with distaste and disfavor any form of open or subtle bullying or browbeating by courts or lawyers. . . . We disapprove of judges who make use of pseudo-Socratic methods more suitable to a law school seminar than to a court for the purpose of embarrassing members of the bar in the presence of

the clients and their colleagues," the appellate court once wrote in a lengthy opinion castigating Beard for his treatment of a lawyer.

Over the years, Beard has developed a reputation among young lawyers as a judge to avoid in the courtroom. Especially among new members of the U. S. Attorney's office he seems to inspire a fear and loathing which was recently put into words by a prosecutor who had spent many hours listening to Beard's haranging.

"It's like being nailed to a cross and stripped naked. You just have to stand there and listen to it and you can't say anything back — if you do you'll go to jail. It's humiliating and emasculating — what else can I say?"[2]

Again, I must point out that this personality is also found in Christians. George and Darlene were a Christian couple whose marriage was falling apart as a result of George's Aggressive Personality. Nothing Darlene did pleased George; he was always fault-finding and critical. Darlene just felt like giving up. There was no pleasing George — why try?

When George was confronted with his hostility, he readily admitted that he was hostile, but according to him, it was justified. He proceeded to list Darlene's faults and capped it off with the observation that he wouldn't be hostile if it were not for Darlene.

The fact of the matter was that George would have found fault with any woman because he needed to. This was his way of establishing his self-worth. His interpersonal message to his wife, and indeed, most of his acquaintances, was, "Watch out; I can be mean!" And to support his game he chose friends, few though they were, who would support his righteous indignation against a wife whose faults were endless.

Another example of this personality is Hank, an intense man who speaks quickly and with great vigor. He was born again at an early age and felt very close to God. He did, however, have difficulty in establishing intimate relations with his peers. This became especially critical in his early teens when he was permitted to skip a grade because of his superior intelligence. Skipping a grade, he found himself still further removed from his classmates. The girls were much more mature, and the guys were less interested in playing ball with him and more interested in the girls.

Both by disposition and position in his peer group, Hank felt different from everyone else. At this critical period his relationship to Christ became very meaningful. He began to find in a deeply religious life a satisfaction that he could not find in his peer group.

The reader will probably stop here and say, "That's great!" But it wasn't so great.

Hank began to rationalize his inability to have meaningful peer relations as a matter of choice on his part. He fancied himself as being very different. He thought of himself as a Christian who wanted to please God. While the other kids were holding hands and kissing, he was determined to "flee youthful lusts."

Again, the reader may say, "Great, Hank. Hang in there!" And this is exactly what the adults of his church did. Hank was the Golden Boy. He was Mr. Clean. While the behavior of the other church kids left something to be desired, Hank emulated all the sterling qualities that a church likes to see in its youth.

Hank began to develop a feeling of self-worth with this "Mr. Clean" image. He was indeed different from all the rest of the youth in his church. He was going to "save himself" for the girl he would marry, an idealized person who would be exactly like him.

As things turned out, he realized that his ideal was unrealistic. There was no such girl, or at least he couldn't find her. He did start dating a girl who moved into his neighborhood at this time. He knew that she liked him, and he thought that he really ought to start dating seriously, because after all, he was twenty-four.

The subsequent courtship was stormy. On one hand he was angry that she didn't "keep herself for him" (she necked with other boys, but was a virgin). On the other hand, her love for him, in spite of his abusive behavior, drew him to her.

Eventually they were married, but immediately the lid blew off the relationship. Hank was angry and unhappy. She had not kept herself for him, yet she seemed to live a contented life. He said, "Here she did all those things with other guys and is in better shape spiritually and emotionally than I am. I'm angry. I'm angry at her and God. It's unfair. I kept myself pure, and she didn't. But I'm more messed up than she is."

The question that seemed to break through the haze was this: "Hank, did you keep yourself 'pure' for *God*, or was this just a rationalization to stay away from girls, whom you felt inadequate with? Hank, it sounds as if you did a real job of conning yourself. You told yourself you didn't touch girls because you were Mr. Clean. This gave you a feeling of superiority and self-worth. You couldn't face the fact that you were really afraid that you'd never get to first base."

Hank was a Pharisee: "I thank God I am not as other men." And he maintained this fiction by outbursts of righteous indignation against his wife for "not keeping herself pure." His self-worth was on the line. No, he could not bear to think that the Publican he was married to was a well-adjusted person. *She didn't keep herself pure!* He had to believe that God was pleased with his White-Knight performance.

As I spoke to Hank, the words of God through the prophet came to mind: "Are you doing all this for me, even for me?" In terms of interpersonal push-pull, the Aggressive Personality pulls resentment, distrust, fear, and guilt from others. The personality most often hooked by him is the modest–Self-Effacing Personality who uses self-depreciation as a means of warding off anxiety. This personality in its extreme form is masochistic. We find with these two personalities the classic sadistic/masochistic relationship. The sadistic Aggressive Personality uses cold, moralistic sternness and punitiveness to demonstrate his uniqueness and, often, moral uprightness. The masochistic Self-Effacing Personality accepts this abuse as an opportunity to demonstrate his harmlessness, and to some degree, to feel worthwhile. In chapter 10, dealing with this personality, we investigate the sadistic/masochistic relationship further.

The pastor and other Christian leaders with an Aggressive Personality will readily draw a following of self-effacing Christians. Their preaching invariably carries punitive and guilt-provoking themes which are advanced, of course, in the name of "faithfulness to the Word." The proclamation of hell-fire, though a proper biblical theme, comes all too frequently and too easily. And the congregation happily comes away each Sunday with the satisfaction that "we are worms."

The depravity of man is indeed an important theme of Scripture. But when it becomes the only theme, or the predominant theme, there is obviously a lack of balance, not only in the personality of the pastor and the individual believers in the church, but also in the collective personality of the church.

The Blunt Personality

The adaptive expression of this personality type is the Blunt Personality. If the Aggressive Personality is to become more adaptive, the following behaviors should be dropped:

Insensitive
Cruel
Harsh and judgmental
Self-righteous
Verbally and physically attacking
Hostility
Verbal abuse
Quarrelsomeness
Excessive strictness and rigidity

Behaviors that should be added to bring this personality into balance are:

Agreeability
Listens to others
Awareness of the feelings of others
Acceptance of others

The Blunt-Aggressive Personality

The Blunt Personality is frank, forthright, mildly critical, direct, and firm in his action. In short, he is aggressive, but the expression of it is milder. His aggressiveness is also tempered by some affectionate traits. He can be gentle, supportive, and sympathetic, though this behavior is not as noticeable as his frankness. When he speaks out he is forthright, but not cutting and destructive like the Aggressive Personality. James and John, the apostles of Jesus, are good examples of the Aggressive Personality's being tempered to a more adaptive form. *Unger's Bible Dictionary* states,

> From the desire to punish the inhabitants of a certain village in Samaria, because they declined to receive Jesus (Luke 9:52-54), we infer that James and John were warm and impetuous in temperament. They were called by our Lord (Mark 3:17) Boanerges — *sons of thunder* — probably on account of their boldness and energy in discharging their apostleship.[3]

John's First Epistle reflects a warmth and tenderness of fifty years of growth following this incident. John speaks tenderly of his "little children" and talks about love.

The Blunt Personality has an important role in keeping balance in the church. When the Overconventional and Hypernormal personalities would deplete the energies and resources of the church through neurotic "do-gooder" schemes, the Blunt Personality is in a good position to objectively separate Christian duty from neurotic, compulsive helpfulness.

In moving Hank from an Aggressive Personality to a Blunt Personality, my first task was to help him see that his Mr. Clean game was not really laudable, but rather lamentable. God never was pleased with Pharisaism in biblical times, and He is not now! It is difficult to move this personality type out of his maladaptive expression of behavior, because he feels he is giving up the uniqueness on which he establishes his self-worth.

Directive counseling, learning contracts, and group exposure are all ways in which this personality can become more adaptive. It should be remembered, however, that in dealing with this personality, warmth and tenderness are threatening. A positive regard for the person is in order without threatening him with too much affection.

It should also be remembered that this personality, much like the Skeptical-Distrustful Personality, needs to feel that he is unique. If his feeling of uniqueness can be preserved in a less hostile frame of reference, he will be more disposed to temper his behavior. In working with him in groups and in learning contracts, it should be remembered that his forthrightness and frankness should be accepted when they are free of hostility and sarcasm. The goal of change will be achieved when the sting is taken out of this personality's directness.

Also helpful in bringing about change in this personality is Publication 512 from the American Institute of Family Relations, entitled "Help for Reducing Hostility." Seventeen specific suggestions are given, among them being:

1. Recognize the feelings you have as they arise. Accept the fact that you have these feelings. Learn not to yield to the temptation of putting your unfriendly or offensive thoughts into words. If you are in a group where criticism is an "indoor sport," refrain from participating in it yourself. Just listen.
2. Realize that your criticism of others often stems from a desire to make yourself feel better. If other people's faults are apparent, one's own don't seem so big. When you can find another person to agree with you about some one else's faults, it is even more reassuring to you.
3. Realize how criticalness can "snowball." Seeing others' faults makes you feel better; but disliking other people makes you dislike yourself and feel disliked by others. This becomes a vicious circle.
4. Be eager to express appreciation and praise whenever you reasonably can. This does not require flattery; appreciation may be given on the basis of what is *good in the circumstances*, rather than what is absolutely superior. For example, you can say *something* gratifying even about an amateur performer in high school dramatics.

The Skeptical-Distrustful Personality

Chapter 9
The Skeptical-Distrustful Personality

THE OUTSTANDING characteristic of the Skeptical-Distrustful Personality is the passive manner by which he creates distance between himself and others. It is similar to the Blunt-Aggressive Personality in that hostility themes are found, but this personality is not as outwardly assertive. It is often called "passive-aggressive" behavior, especially when found in its maladaptive form. It is aggressive because it is hostile, but it is passive because the hostility is expressed in a more covert manner. This person does not attack; he is more likely to rebel, and if maladaptive, he may even sabotage or simply become an immovable object.

In my counseling practice I have noticed that a high percentage of overweight clients fall into this personality type. It is as though obesity facilitates the reduction of anxiety by making self immovable. It seems likely, though, that obesity would present problems with self-image. And it does. But the obese passive-aggressive person often solves his dilemma by making excuses or by seeing himself as a unique individual and taking pride in his "size."

It should be remembered that interpersonal behavior is aimed at *reducing* anxiety. Those who feel badly about their obesity imagine that obesity is not so bad as being pushed around. If becoming an immovable object keeps this personality from being pushed around, there is some benefit to it. Not only that, the obese person often sees himself as being "thickskinned," and indeed, he is. Studies by Dr. Alexander Lowen (*Betrayal of the Body*, Macmillan) reveal that we muster our muscle systems to defend ourselves. We tense certain parts of our body to cope with anxiety. On this theoretical base Dr. Lowen has developed a therapy called "bioenergetics," which has proved highly effective.

I suggest, following Lowen's theory, that many obese people actually make themselves "thickskinned" through overeating as a way to protect themselves against anxiety. The extra fat serves the same purpose that tense muscle systems serve — to protect against hurt. It should follow, then, that when this personality learns to cope with anxiety in more adaptive ways, there should be no more need for a "thick skin," and the passive-aggressive obese person should benefit from weight loss by dealing with the anxiety more constructively.

The Distrustful Personality

The maladaptive form for this person is the Distrustful Personality. Again, attitude is the key. It is cynical, passively resistant and bitter. These persons reduce their anxiety by establishing distance between themselves and others.

It seems likely that the cultural and Christian ideals of closeness and cooperation would make them see their lack of adjustment. Yet in their personality development they have found that closeness and positive feelings can be traumatic. They carry these feelings over into adulthood and protect themselves by keeping people at a distance with their passively negative attitude. Though they may not like the rejection, and indeed may long for warmth and tenderness, they still provoke

The Skeptical-Distrustful Personality

rejection from others. It is not a conscious act on their part, but rather an involuntary reflex in the interest of self-protection.

This personality type exhibits sour, pessimistic or indifferent feelings. Often this is seen in flat affect of voice or in an apparent absence of feelings. Their behavior seems to be saying, "I am a sullen, disappointed person; you can't do anything for me." This personality is very sensitive to phoniness, pomposity, and arrogance in others, and he looks for dishonesty and hostility in others.

Though the behavior of this personality type is bound to pull hostility from others, he still engages in this behavior as his "security operation." What does he hope to accomplish? At least two things.

The first is self-worth. This personality fancies himself a unique individual. He rejects conventionality. His rebellion demonstrates that he will not permit himself to be stamped out of the same mold that all the other "plastic people" come from.

The second is deliverance from the anxiety created by his tender feelings. Often this personality has repeatedly experienced rejection when expressing tender feelings. In the process of growing up he has come to equate tender feelings in himself with the anxiety of rejection by others. Rather than expose those tender feelings to the danger of hurt, he covers them with a sullen facade. By giving an "I don't care about you" message he heads off the danger of having his loving feelings hurt — he isn't showing loving feelings, but just the opposite — and while his defenses are up, he precipitates rejection, which he imagines is there all the time. He feels that he just "gets it over with." Leary says about this behavior,

> The severely distrustful person is most comfortable when he is expressing bitter feelings. He is threatened and suspicious of tenderness which can be viewed as an intolerable threat to his mode of adjustment. This common assumption that what the deprived, distrustful person needs is love and affection can be seen to be a well-meaning but naive notion. To the person with a set of severely crippled reflexes tenderness in the "other one" is a loaded gun — a most frightening and fearful stimulus. . . .

D. H. Lawrence has provided us with a clear illustration of the way in which the distrustful, disaffiliated person avoids tender feelings. The hero of *Aaron's Rod* announces: "I don't want my Fate or my Providence to treat me well. I don't want kindness or love. I don't believe in harmony and people loving one another. I believe in the fight and in nothing else. I believe in the fight which is in everything. And if it is a question of women, I believe in the fight of love, even if it blinds me. And if it is a question of the world, I believe in fighting it and in having it hate me, even if it breaks my leg. I want the world to hate me, because I can't bear the thought that it might love me. For of all things love is the most deadly to me, and especially from such a repulsive world as I think this is. . . ."[1]

The implications of this for the Christian trying to live the Christian life are tremendous. How is it possible for him to live and work in a community of believers that ostensibly is committed to loving behavior? The answer to that question is, "Not very well." Such was the case of Jerry, a young seminary student.

I was approached by Jerry after a speaking engagement in the seminary chapel. He said that he liked many of the things I said and admired my sincerity, but he had some problems with the kind of warm, loving Christianity I had talked about.

We went out for coffee, and soon he was spilling out his venom about the seminary. He wanted me to know about the hypocrisy and stupidity of the people there, and how they were keeping him from living the kind of Christian life God wanted him to live. They were all "hung up on traditionalism," according to Jerry, and he wasn't going to become a plastic person like the rest of the compliant student body.

Jerry repeatedly had been in trouble with the seminary administration for his noncooperation. He was a rebel, and he laughed with delight about the things that he did to annoy the administration. But finally he was asked to leave school.

I got to know Jerry well. We spent many hours together socially, and it was in this kind of intimacy that I noticed something interesting about his behavior. Every so often he

The Skeptical-Distrustful Personality

would do or say something outrageous that seemed to be testing me. I had told him that I loved him, and he seemed greatly to enjoy my company. At first his behavior baffled me: if he enjoyed my company, why did he act as though he wanted to drive me away? Leary says malevolence like this can be seen as asking the question, "Even if I do this and am like this, can you still love me?" There seems to be a violent testing of the one who professes love with anticipation that the answer will come, "No, the other cannot love." When rejection does not come, there is further negativistic testing and at the same time the continued hope of finally finding the one who will not reject.

What a tragic dilemma for the Distrustful Personality. He tries to set to rest his anxiety about rejection by testing love with outrageous behavior, and yet it is that very behavior that brings about rejection.

Dealing with this behavior was difficult for Jerry, but we finally used the contract method. I told him, "Jerry, if I feel that you're testing my love, I will say so and you are to agree to stop the testing. In return, I agree to show you my love in those off moments when you are not testing it." By identifying the testing behavior when it occurred, I was able to render Jerry an important service in helping him overcome it. By showing him my love unexpectedly, I didn't give him an opportunity to thwart it by resistant, skeptical, or sour behavior.

Sometimes the Distrustful Personality manifests his distrust by avoiding eye contact. When there is eye contact, it is often a distrustful, sideward glance. Joan's eye contact was marked with this peculiarity. When I called it to her attention, she was quite surprised. I suggested that she might be able to deal with her distrust by coping directly with this distrustful behavior, and she agreed to contract with me on this. I was to call it to her attention whenever she did it, and she was to respond by looking me directly in the eye. When she did this, it put her in touch with feelings of distrust and their roots. She expected to be hurt by others, and it was out of this expectation that she manifested the distrust in her eyes. By having her talk about her trust of me, or lack of it, I forced her to deal more directly with her anxiety. With this directness, she was able to alter her passive behavior; by her being open about the feelings she feared and by not experiencing attack for revealing them, she began to drop some of her hostility.

When it comes to interpersonal push-pull, the Distrustful Personality is a master at provoking others into punishing behavior. He provokes to impatience or moral censure. Such was the case with Jerry. He, of course, justified his behavior on the ground that he was resisting something that was unreasonable, and to some extent, what he felt was a perversion of what God really wanted a seminary to be. This carried back to the idea of a uniqueness that Jerry thought he had.

It is readily seen that this can degenerate into a "martyr complex." The Distrustful Personality may feel himself very spiritual for having suffered the wounds of "the establishment." I never cease to be amazed at how Christians with a maladaptive personality can justify themselves on spiritual grounds, no matter what type of maladaptive personality they might have.

The Skeptical Personality

In moving the Distrustful Personality to a more adaptive form, the Skeptical Personality, the following behaviors are to be purged from the personality:

> Extreme cynicism
> Constant fault-finding
> Jealousy
> An unforgiving spirit
> Never believing anything that is said
> Distrust

The following behaviors should be added to the personality:

> Sympathetic
> Generous
> Giving of self
> Comforting

Forgiving
Accepting of others

One of the most memorable changes of this personality from its maladaptive to its adaptive form was seen in Chuck. Though he was a successful young engineer, Chuck was never happy about the way things went either on the job or at home. His main complaint was with his home life. He had composed a long catalog of his wife's faults. The outstanding feature of Chuck's personality was his fault-finding.

A pattern in his behavior quickly emerged. Whenever he was feeling down on himself, he made himself feel better by scapegoating his wife. He imagined that if it weren't for her, things would be much better for him. But in fact, her behavior had little to do with his unhappiness; he was looking in the wrong direction. He was really unhappy with himself and sought release through fault-finding.

By my getting Chuck and his wife into a learning contract she was able to help him monitor his behavior and counter it by being more accepting of her and sharing with her whatever made him unhappy with himself. By accepting the responsibility for his own unhappiness he forced himself to do something constructive about the circumstances that were making him unhappy. He continued to maintain a mild skepticism, which made his research work very productive — he was able to do the unconventional in engineering research and design. But he dropped the extreme criticalness that ruined relations with his wife.

Moving the Distrustful Personality to its less extreme form, the Skeptical Personality, may not seem like much of an improvement. The term *skeptical,* unfortunately, has all too often a negative connotation. But there are redeeming qualities in the Skeptical Personality. A *healthy* critical approach to convention is important to keeping the individual or the organization he works for from getting into a rut. The Skeptical Personality is not afraid to do the unconventional, which many times leads to new breakthroughs in personal and organizational effectiveness. Often creative people have this kind of health; not bound by fear of bucking convention, their minds are free to explore alternative approaches to life and work. I have had a few inventors as clients, and they seem to cluster around this personality type.

I do not mean to imply that the Christian is to cast off the restrictions of Scripture. But such people often have a true appreciation of Christian liberty.

Skepticism also is excellent protection against surprises. Some skeptics adopt a *mildly* disappointed cynicism as protection against future disappointments. But the emphasis on "mildly" should be noted. Again, the Christian life is one of balance. Mild skepticism serves this person as well as the mild optimism that serves the Responsible Personality. Leary notes,

> The critical, rebellious person can play a most healthy role in any social group. Docile inertia or fearful-need-to-conform or need-to-be-liked can lead to a stultifying atmosphere. There are valuable rewards for the successful rebel who maintains a realistic, accurate skepticism toward the accepted ways of doing things. . . .
>
> [This] mode of adjustment has been eulogized by many writers. Its most enthusiastic advocate is Robert Lindner. He states: "It is possible, then, to escape from history, to break out of the cage whose outer limits never have worn smooth and deeply grooved with endless pacing. And it is possible to do this without the letting of blood, without violence, without the sacrifice of basic values. All that is required is to reach for one cup wherein the heady mixture of true rebellion, the brew of sweet life-affirming protest, has been poured, for *this* — and this alone — is the *elixir vitae*."[2]

It is going a bit far to make this personality the paragon of mental health. We must remember that there are at least eight personality types, each with an adaptive expression. This is what makes interpersonal relations such a delightful experience and serious study. Variety does indeed keep matters interesting, and it is this variety that provides very effective interpersonal complementariness when both personalities are adaptive.

The Modest-Self-Effacing Personality

Chapter 10
The Modest-Self-Effacing Personality

"I AM A WEAK, harmless person. You need not fear me. In fact, I'm really a stupid person. Let me demonstrate my stupidity to you." This is the interpersonal message of the Self-Effacing Personality. In its more adaptive form, the Modest Personality, the message is not so self-deprecating. This person is feeling safest when he conveys the message that he does not have too much going for him. He imagines that if he assumes an absolutely nonthreatening posture, he will not be hurt. Here once again we see the reduction of anxiety as the motive for interpersonal behavior.

THE SELF-EFFACING PERSONALITY

This personality is the polar opposite of the Autocratic Personality that says, "You can't hurt me." This personality says, "Please don't hurt me. I'm harmless. You need not worry about me."

It should be noted, however, that the person who employs this method of reducing anxiety does not always respond the same way in every situation. When he is with people he feels safe with, he may appear less embarrassed and retiring. He usually employs these defenses in the presence of those who are strong.

The outstanding symptom of this personality is depression. He is anxious, unhappy, and guilt-ridden. He is passive and immobile. He is not active, self-confident, or assertive.

In its maladaptive form this personality is masochistic. Without going into the psychiatric ramifications of masochism, I should say simply that this individual has grown up with the message that he is unlovable. He carries on the game of being as unlovable as others expect him to be. By meeting this expectation he reduces his anxiety.

Where does self-worth come in? How can such a person get a feeling of self-worth? It comes by imagining he is pleasing others at the expense of his own interests. In terms of transactional analysis he takes the position, "You're OK; I'm not OK." Though his role in life is a hard one, the masochist feels he is fulfilling his unique role of suffering to make others happy.

George was a clear example of the Self-Effacing Personality. When he first came for counseling, I recall feeling annoyed at his continually showering me with praise and his running himself down. This was my clue to his complaint that nothing ever worked out for him — that he always seemed to be the victim of circumstances.

The fact of the matter is that George couldn't afford to succeed. After all, if he did succeed he might be a threat to others. But by always being a doormat he was no threat.

He also had the ability to talk without saying anything. At first I thought something was wrong with my mental processes: it sounded like a schizoid defense. As long as George didn't say anything comprehensible, he could not be held accountable for saying anything that offended! Whenever I called this to his attention, he lapsed into self-reproach.

His favorite pasttime was the "idiot game." He portrayed himself as an absolute idiot anytime he felt threatened with

The Modest-Self-Effacing Personality

confrontation by people he was not secure with. He could be direct and hostile toward his wife and children, with whom he felt safe; but with a counselor or others whom he regarded as a threat, he would lapse into his game.

George's behavior is more understandable when seen in the larger context of clowning behavior. The clown or social buffoon forces others to laugh at him and patronize him. And when he is patronized, he feels he is in a more secure position. This is, however, at the cost of self-worth.

I suspect that sometimes those who earn their living as comedians might have gotten their start by handling anxiety in just this manner. Being a comedian is fine, as long as a person doesn't carry his self-deprecating behavior over into all interpersonal relationships.

Interestingly, while hostility is not too evident on the Interpersonal Adjective Check List, this personality scores high in hostility on the Taylor-Johnson Temperament Analysis. The reason seems to be that this person's hostility is toward someone not present. However, if that person *were* present, the hostility would go unexpressed, and the self-effacer would take the blame for any trouble between them and feel extremely guilty for even complaining. This personality deals with his hostility by turning it on himself. He cannot bring himself to turn it against others he feels threatened by. One of his major problems is a lack of assertiveness — something that can be corrected by assertive training.

From this it is easily seen why this personality commonly suffers depression. He continually punishes himself, and his body, unable to take this punishment, anesthetizes itself against the pain with the numbness of depression. This, of course, presents the self-effacer with a real problem: shall he suffer the anxiety of being more assertive, or shall he face the depression that comes from being totally unassertive?

When this personality is found in the Christian, it is extremely difficult to deal with, since self-effacing conduct is often thought to be Christian behavior. At this point I must distinguish between self-effacing behavior and modesty. The modest person is able to criticize himself without going to the extreme of being self-punishing, which the self-effacing person is guilty of. It's a matter of degree. When the self-effacer reads his Bible and comes across all the exhortations to modesty, he revels in it; he finds support for his maladaptive personality. When he sings that old hymn "At the Cross," he relishes the line "Would He devote that sacred head/For such a worm as I?" Not only does he find satisfaction at being the kind of worm his parents taught him to be, but now he can be the worm the great hymnwriters want him to be. Certainly God wants us to take a modest view of ourselves. But God does not want neurotic children immobilized by self-depreciation, doubt, rumination, and uncertainty.

Russ Llewellyn, in *Action* magazine, produced a great essay on this subject entitled "Down With the Worm!" He said,

> Jesus taught the value of man. He comforted those who despaired of their worth, saying, "You can buy two sparrows for a penny; yet not a single one of them falls to the ground without your Father's consent. As for you, even the hairs of your head have all been counted. So do not be afraid; you are worth much more than sparrows" (Matt. 10:29-31).[1]

He added that Psalm 22, a Messianic Psalm, teaches us that when Jesus said, "I am a worm and no man," He let us know that in order to be despised as worthless He had to be treated as less than a man — a worm.

> *That God created man in His image provides unimpeachable evidence that man is valuable.* James recognized this when he condemned the cursing of people because man is made after the likeness of God. Moses [sic] provided capital punishment on this premise: "Whoso sheddeth man's blood, by man shall his blood be shed; for in the image of God made he man."
>
> Man's worth is an inherent, created worth. God guaranteed the recognition of this when he fixed the penalty that life must be forfeited when life is taken.[2]

To use Christianity to bolster a maladaptive personality is

The Modest-Self-Effacing Personality

spiritually sick behavior. But because this behavior resembles the Christian ideal of modesty, the self-effacer is permitted to continue his sick behavior in the church.

The Self-Effacing Personality (which I have identified as masochistic) most readily hooks into the Aggressive Personality (which tends to be sadistic). Each performs for the other a service. The Aggressive Personality is able to deal with his hostility by unloading it on the Self-Effacing Personality. The Self-Effacing Personality deals with his hostility by directing it at himself and thereby becomes the despised creature that he thinks will please everyone. By permitting this introjected hostility to create depression, he can truly feel that he is what he thinks others want him to be — a nothing!

The Modest Personality

In order to move the Self-Effacing Personality to its more adaptive form, the Modest Personality, the following behaviors must be dropped:

> Extreme manifestations of weakness
> Lack of verbal and physical assertiveness
> Self-depreciation
> Extreme self-criticism
> Continual rumination about right and wrong
> Acceptance of depression as an excuse for immobility
> Giving in too easily

These behaviors must be substituted with polar behaviors of strength and assertiveness:

> Speaking louder and more rapidly
> Walking with a brisker step
> Playing with vigor in competitive games
> Insisting on his own way or point of view
> Refusing to give in all the time
> Taking the lead in conversation or action

In dealing with George, I called to his attention the necessity for trial — trial that would force him to change. When George could see that he needed to be more assertive and less self-punishing, he would be better able to understand the trials that God put him through. Our trials from God are designed to make our maladaptive security operations unworkable, forcing us into trying more adaptive, coping behavior. When adaptive behaviors are reinforced by people close to us, we most likely will continue in that new conduct. It helps to know what we're looking for. It is a great improvement on random trial and error.

George could expect to go through experiences in which his self-effacing behavior would not protect him. I told him that when this happened he would probably step up his self-effacing behavior, thinking he was not self-effacing enough. God's trial would be engineered in such a marvelous way that no matter how self-effacing he was, he still would be plagued with anxiety and still would not be pleasing to others. When he came to that place, he was to take the responsibility for acting more assertively and to seek God's wisdom in acting more assertively (James 1:5,6).

I cannot emphasize enough the necessity of trial. God must render our maladaptive security operation ineffective if we are to be motivated to behave differently.

When George knew what to expect in terms of trial — and that trial at the hands of a loving God — he was better able to cooperate with fellow-believers who loved him and wanted to facilitate change. It must be remembered that people are the sandpaper of life that God uses to knock off the rough edges, so to talk about "facilitating" the divine process is not presumptuous. It is to be expected. Here, of course, is where believers need to be spiritually sensitive to God's working and available to be used. We need to see that sometimes the pain we create in the lives of other believers may not be wholly bad.

Too often believers suppose that the pain they create in the lives of others *is* bad, and they actually disobey God when they refuse to be part of the process. It was this very response that

The Modest-Self-Effacing Personality

kept other believers from helping George to change. George would normally attempt to pull dominant-hostile behavior from others so he could play his self-effacing game. When he did this, they would feel that they had done an unchristian thing and then either apologize to George and get on a merry-go-round of game-playing with him, or withdraw in frustration. George had total control of the situation.

With George I attempted to develop assertiveness in him both verbally and physically. It was understood that we needed to break up the usual game of his acting like underdog and thrusting me into a topdog role. When he would start playing the self-effacing game I would identify it. I would also identify the natural response of others — to come on strong and dominate him. Having identified the game, I would go ahead and play it to the hilt, identifying what I was doing and pointing out how he was devouring it.

Then I asked him to reverse roles. I told him that I wanted him to be assertive and silence me. I would dominate until he moved in on me and silenced me. All he had to do to silence me was say, "I've heard enough; be quiet," and it had to be said in firm tones. He was so committed to his self-effacing game that even when I invited him to silence me, he would not. His first few attempts were very timid, but with encouragement he got used to hearing his voice speaking firm, direct language.

The second step in reconditioning George's self-effacing behavior was to make him comfortable with hitting motions. Hitting motions are aggressive moves, something uncomfortable to the Self-Effacing Personality. I use a padded bat called a "Bataca." I encouraged him simply to go through the motions of hitting an empty chair: he did it weakly and timidly. I finally was able to get him up to administering some hard blows to the chair, even though the sound was frightening to him. He grew accustomed to making aggressive moves without fear of reprisal.

The next step was to get George into a learning contract with his wife. Whenever George criticized himself, gave in too easily, or showered others with inappropriate compliments, she was to call it to his attention, and he was to stop the behavior and substitute it with polar behavior — more assertiveness. She was to watch out for his game of pulling punishment from her. He could always manage to behave in such a way as to cause her to emasculate him.

The most profound effect on George occurred in the Communication Workshop. He tried his best to play the clown and get the others to laugh at and patronize him. But when the group facilitator began to probe George, the meaning of his behavior soon became evident. The group refused to let George put himself down. They turned a deaf ear to his self-deprecation and would hear him and become warm only when he had something good to say about himself.

At first George was very frustrated. His usual security operation was not working. But he soon became comfortable with a more positive view of himself, and gradually he was able to share his hostility directly with members of the group who troubled him, rather than turn the hostility on himself and blame himself for "not getting along."

The group also handled George's depression well. George could easily monopolize the entire group session by being depressed and pulling dominant attempts to get him out of his depression. In the earlier sessions the groups took on the mentality, "Let's make George feel good." But it soon became evident that if they really succeeded in making George feel good, he would no longer be the center of attention, so he really couldn't afford to let them make him feel good. When this was pointed out by the facilitator, the group refused to be hooked. If George came in with his glum look, he found himself in a bind. Either he had to lie about his mood and report that he was feeling fine when he didn't look like it, or he had to report that he was depressed and go through the agony of having no one play "Let's make George feel good." In fact, rather than taking on the responsibility of making him feel good, the group wanted to know what *he* was doing about his problem.

The Modest-Self-Effacing Personality

The American Institute of Family Relations has a number of publications used in conjunction with the Taylor-Johnson Temperament Analysis, publications that suggest ways for changing specific traits, such as Publication 513, "Suggestions for Decreasing Depression." It should be remembered, however, that many times the Self-Effacing Personality will not do what can be done to get himself out of depression because he *needs* to be depressed. Depression actually facilitates his game. Those who are continually depressed need to face squarely the fact that they may well be getting something out of their depression. It may be facilitating a maladaptive security operation.

The Docile-Dependent Personality

Chapter 11
The Docile-Dependent Personality

THE DOCILE-DEPENDENT Personality differs from the Modest-Self–Effacing personality primarily in the degree of affection that is expressed. Docile-Dependent Personality is more affectionate, though this affection is usually not evident in the maladaptive form of this personality, dependence.

THE DEPENDENT PERSONALITY

The Dependent Personality is a meek conformist. He conveys the message (though more often it is "she") "I am a meek, admiring person in need of your help and advice." Frequently this personality wears a fixed smile inappropriate for the circumstances. The "smile mask" is not unique to this personality, however; it is often found in the Overconventional and Overgenerous Personalities. It is an outward manifestation of maladaptive affection common to these personalities.

This personality finds that he is able to handle his anxiety best by pulling help from those whom he perceives as strong. There is also a certain amount of self-worth obtained by this behavior. He finds himself the object of care and concern by someone else, often someone of repute.

He does not always behave in this manner. Again, when he feels safe, he may not be so meek and compliant. This is why maladaptive personalities are often confused when told by a counselor that they are behaving maladaptively. They often reply, "My friends don't think I do." In all likelihood, the friends say this because the behavior really is different around them. But in society at large, the Dependent Personality will behave in his typically maladaptive way when confronted by those whom he feels are strong and threatening. Under those circumstances he appears helpless, painful, uncertain, frightened, hopeless, dependent, and passive.

This person can be a "bottomless pit," a real problem-child in the church. No matter how much help, encouragement, or prayer is offered on behalf of the Dependent Personality, nothing seems to help. He unconsciously feels he cannot afford to be cured. If he is cured, he will not have any reason to pull help from strong others, an interpersonal relationship that he finds comfortable.

The fears of the dependent person are displaced fears. Often unconscious fears of father or mother are displaced to other persons or stimuli. For example, this free-floating anxiety may attach itself to fear of heights, to fear of some physical ailment, or to some vague unknown person or object.

The Dependent Personality discovers in the process of growing up that he is least anxious when being lovingly submissive to parents in spite of hurt or anxiety he may experience at their hands. Because he cannot bring himself to dislike hurtful parents or be assertive toward them, he displaces his fear to a more acceptable object, or a fearful unknown object. He cannot bring himself to express fear of parent. But he may express fear of something else.

Dependent behavior is often encouraged by tyrannical parents. The child finds them less fearful when he behaves in a meek, helpless manner. They back off when the child behaves in

The Docile-Dependent Personality

this manner and thus reinforce anxious, helpless behavior.

The Dependent Personality is a good candidate for troublesome physical symptoms:

1. *Anxiety Neurosis*. This disturbance expresses itself in attacks of vague, unexplained, but intense fear, which is usually not attached to any particular object. The person may even show symptoms found in the expression of real fear — cold sweat and palpitation of the heart. He may fear that his heart will stop or something will burst in his head.

2. *Neurasthenia*. This condition is characterized by feelings of physical and mental inadequacy, complaints of fatigue without adequate exertion, and strange tingling sensations in the back of the neck.

The implications of disorders rising out of the Dependent Personality are great for the Christian. The Dependent Personality is attempting to cope with anxiety by (1) expressing dependence and need for help, and (2) displacing negative emotions to physical reactions. But by doing this he runs into conflict with biblical teachings about spiritual maturity, teachings that encourage "Cast all your care on Jesus for he cares for you" and "Stop being anxious about everything. . . ." (cf. 1 Peter 5:7; Phil. 4:6). The Dependent Personality says, "I know all this! How do I stop?" The fact is, he really doesn't want to hear the answer to that question. The answer involves behavior he does not want to give up — dependent, helpless, weak, trustful behavior. He may have to face the fact that the real fear is fear of parent which has been displaced to something else. He may be asked to face this fear that he has repressed for so long.

This person, who often seems highly motivated for counseling, may begin to resist when these issues are brought into focus and he begins to give rationalizations. "It's not Christian to express anger with one's parents. The Bible says to honor father and mother" and so forth. In actuality, he doesn't want to face the *real* feared object.

Such a reaction sets up a pattern of seeking help and

ultimately rejecting that help and moving on to someone else. On the superficial level it appears that this person is actually using his ills to establish social bonds with others. I say "on a superficial level," because the Dependent Personality doesn't really understand the dynamics of what is happening. All he knows is that the pain is relieved when he is with helpful others. So long as he is with helpful others he feels good, and soon this becomes a way of life. He spends his entire life seeking out such people and never really solving his problems. The church offers a wonderful resource for this personality: there are many nutrient, strong, helpful, responsible individuals in the church who feel it's their Christian duty to help. Soon these helpful people — who tend to be Overgenerous Personalities — are hooked into a relationship with the Dependent Personality, who eventually drains the Overgenerous Personality dry. The Overgenerous Personality knows that something's wrong with the relationship, but can't bring himself to say to the Dependent Personality, "It seems that no matter how much help is given, it really doesn't solve your problems." Even if he were to say this, the dependent one would give assurances that the overgenerous one is very helpful — and the game goes on *ad nauseum*. If the overgenerous one wants to get out of this sick relationship, the dependent one can make him feel guilty for "abandoning someone in need."

I must stress the fact that the Dependent Personality, in terms of neurotic behavior, unconsciously *needs* his anxiety and physical symptoms. They are his defense against anxiety. They provide an opportunity for a nurturable person to give him the message "You're worthy of my attention," which is a boost to self-worth.

Cindy is an example of the Dependent Personality. When she sought counseling, her presenting complaint was depression and anxiety. It was a classic anxiety neurosis. She was afraid she would stop breathing, and she became very conscious of every breath she took.

In working through her depression and anxiety Cindy

The Docile-Dependent Personality

discovered that she had much fear of her father. She found it difficult to face this fear and would rather talk about her "real" problem, her anxiety about breathing. She portrayed her father as a good Christian and a loving person. But when I pressed her on this matter, she admitted that she never really felt loved by him. Her real feeling was fear of him.

On the interpersonal level she seemed to be reaching out for a father-figure to love her. She was adept at hooking older men into a supportive relationship, which she and they excused as filling the need for "Christian fatherly love" that she never got from her father. But in fact the love was not very "fatherly": Cindy had several close brushes with sexual involvement, which threw her into even greater depression. She was sure that God was punishing her for sinful thoughts about these men, and for sexual thoughts about her own father. She was certain that one day she simply would not be able to breathe.

I should add this about the Dependent Personality: those who are required to counsel this personality must be extremely careful not to be hooked into a manipulation. Though this personality does not consciously plead for help, the body is in an unconscious conspiracy to produce symptoms that most normal people would respond to. For example, this personality may produce extreme disorientation or fainting spells as a way of stepping up his game. In dealing with Cindy I made it very clear that I would do no more for her than I would do for any other client, and if she became disoriented or produced any other symptoms of complete helplessness, I would have her hospitalized. The Dependent Personality cannot be permitted to control the family or counselor by symptoms of helplessness.

In short, Cindy presented a great challenge. She was a classic Dependent Personality, complete with anxiety neurosis, who needed to move to a more adaptive expression of her personality, the Docile Personality.

THE DOCILE PERSONALITY

Cindy had both a spiritual and emotional problem that

needed to be solved. It was interesting to see how she resisted the solution. When I dealt with forgiveness by and fellowship with God the Father, she had many reasons why this couldn't possibly work for her. It mattered not what theological reasons I mustered — she always had an excuse for remaining the unforgiven, "scarlet" woman.

My intuition began to sense that she really couldn't afford to be forgiven. If she felt forgiven, she would begin to solve her problems, which would rob her of my support and that of her friends. Moreover, if she felt forgiven she would have no excuse to fear that God would make her stop breathing. She then would have to look at the *real* fear she was displacing — something she didn't want to do. She found it painful to talk about her fear of her father and deal directly with that.

As an aside, I find again and again that people who fear God in a neurotic way tend to carry a great deal of fear for their earthly father. Conversely, those who have had a good relationship with an earthly father tend to have the same good feelings about God.

For behavioral change Cindy needed to drop the following behaviors:

> Extreme dependency
> Letting others take care of all of her needs
> Unwillingness to make decisions
> Unwillingness to talk back
> Believing anyone
> Behaving like a parasite
> Perpetual child

Behaviors she needed to develop were these:

> Independence
> Assertiveness
> Competitiveness
> Make own decisions
> Express feelings and opinions
> Value her own importance

The Docile-Dependent Personality

In bringing about these changes, I called to her attention the necessity of first recognizing what behavior needed changing in her life and then remembering the divine methodology of bringing about change: trial. If she really wanted to change, Cindy was to expect trial. This was the most fearful part of the process. Whenever she shrank from the prospect of trial, I suggested that perhaps she liked herself the way she was. She emphatically replied that nothing could be worse than her present state of mind. The pain of her maladaptive personality finally was giving her motivation for change.

I pointed out that when trial came, she was to receive it as opportunity to change. She knew she must behave more assertively. She was to examine the trial for opportunities to act more assertively and to pray for wisdom in exercising this.

I cannot stress enough the divine method of change. Often Christians pray for relief from their distress without realizing the terms of relief. The Christian who is aware of what needs to be changed is in a good position to benefit intelligently from trial. He is able to see the purpose of trial when he understands what God is trying to change in him.

To promote the divine process for change in Cindy, I resorted to the three-fold procedure I usually follow.

The first was directive counseling. Whenever Cindy behaved dependently, I called it to her attention and asked her to express herself more assertively. For example, a typical way of expressing nonassertive behavior was her continual smile. Whenever she smiled inappropriately, I would call it to her attention and ask her not to smile. She had an extremely difficult time suppressing it; for one complete session I had her physically restrain the smile by pushing the corners of her mouth together with her hand. At first this produced tears. She felt anxious when forced not to smile (this demonstrated how she used her smile to hold back anxiety). By treating her kindly when she did not smile — a procedure followed for several sessions — I reinforced what I was saying: she didn't have to smile all the time in order to be safe with others.

She also tended to talk in a quiet tone as though not to offend. I encouraged her to talk more assertively, first by raising the volume of her voice. I tape-record all my sessions, and my recorder has a visual sound meter. I asked her to count from one to ten and recite the alphabet loud enough to raise the indicator to an acceptable level. At first she found it difficult to raise her voice. But through repeated attempts she was able to register an acceptable sound level and become used to hearing her voice with a more assertive volume.

Assertive training is being used by many Christian counselors as a practical way of dealing with this type of personality. Edward W. C. McAllister writes in the *Journal of Psychology and Theology*, "Many Christians are in need of assertive training because they view being nonassertive as part of their Christianity. This may be particularly true of women." He then quotes Wolpe's adoption of Salter's six modes of behavior for assertive training:

1. *Feeling Talk* — By this Salter means the deliberate use of spontaneously felt emotions. An example he gives is, "Thank heavens, today is Friday and the weekend is here," in contrast to saying dryly, "Today is Friday."
2. *Facial Talk* — This is the display of emotion in face and movement as far as it is appropriate.
3. *Contradict and Attack* — When the patient disagrees with someone, he is not to pretend agreement, but to contradict with as much feeling as is reasonable.
4. *The Use of I* — The word "I" is used as much as possible so as to involve the patient in the statements he makes.
5. *Express Agreement When You Are Praised* — Praise should not be warded off, but accepted honestly. Self-praise should also be volunteered when reasonable.
6. *Improvise* — Try to make spontaneous response to an immediate stimulus.[1]

McAllister also quotes a number of biblical examples of this type of assertiveness: Feeling Talk, Mark 3:1-6; 9:17-19; 10:13-15; Facial Talk, Mark 10:20-32; Contradict and Attack,

The Docile-Dependent Personality

Mark 2:23-27; The Use of I, Mark 3:13-15.

The second step in the process of facilitating the divine methodology is learning contracts. I encouraged Cindy to make learning contracts with close friends who were to help her monitor her dependent actions and reinforce the expression of more assertive behavior.

The third step was to place her in a group. Cindy was encouraged to practice expressing her assertiveness in the group. One group member was a high-ranking government worker who was having problems with the opposite personality type: he was an Exploitive Personality. I could tell that Cindy was deathly afraid of him. Whenever he spoke, she would put on her smile and be very agreeable. I knew this was a facade to cover her fear of him.

During one session, when Exploitive was boring in with his usual dominant-hostile behavior, I asked Cindy what she thought about him. She attempted to take the dependent, agreeable nonaggressive role. I could tell that she really wasn't as agreeable as she professed to be; a bit of probing brought tears of fear and an expression of resentment toward Exploitive. In the interaction that followed, these two personalities — polar opposites — knocked some of the rough edges off each other. Exploitive saw how he intimidated others, and Cindy saw how she permitted herself to be cowed by a dominant personality.

I repeat that people are the sandpaper of life that God uses to smooth off our rough edges.

As Cindy became familiar with more assertive behavior and was positively reinforced in it, she was more willing to face her real fear, her father. I encouraged her to engage in correspondence with him and express her real feelings to him, which was an assertive behavior. In her earlier letters she would say what she thought he wanted to hear. So at first her more assertive letters brought an attack from father: he wanted to know what was wrong with her. What was this sudden expression of hostility and resentment? Many times she would come for counseling in tears, ready to give in, unable to face her father's counterattack. But by my coaching her over a period of time in how to be assertive in a Christian way, she eventually was able to get her father to accept her feelings.

There are many Cindys in the church suffering anxiety and feeling terribly unspiritual because Christians are not supposed to be anxious. I ask the other Cindys in the church to consider the possibility that their anxiety may not be a spiritual problem; it may well be the result of a maladaptive expression of their personality. Docile? Yes. Dependent? No.

The Cooperative-Overconventional Personality

Chapter 12
The Cooperative-Overconventional Personality

CHRISTIANS WHO must live and work with those who have an Overconventional Personality face a unique problem. The problem is that this personality seems to be so close to the cultural and Christian ideal.

THE OVERCONVENTIONAL PERSONALITY

Persons who compulsively and repetitiously smile, agree, collaborate, conciliate, and are extroverted and outgoing to an intense degree are described as having an Overconventional Personality. They are rigidly friendly, strive to please, and go so far in attempting to establish good relations with others that they seem to have no opinions or desires of their own. They cannot tolerate hostility or assertiveness in themselves and others and are so rigidly committed to affiliable behavior that they often misinterpret hostile intent — they just don't see it.

Even when suffering the pain of hostile behavior at the hands of others, these persons prefer not to acknowledge the hostility or the hurt. They leave the field of action and forget the wrongdoing or justify the behavior of the person who has hurt them. As a result, this personality tends to be bland, naive, and uninsightful.

When this personality is found in the Christian home or church, it presents a unique problem to family and friends who must deal with him. The Christian with the personality finds it convenient to do what we saw was typical of the Docile-Dependent Personality: he uses Christian ideals as justification for his behavior. He will ask, "Isn't a Christian supposed to smile, agree, collaborate, and conciliate?" The answer is obvious: a Christian is to seek peace with all men. But what this personality does not understand is the qualification that the apostle Paul made when he said, "As much as lieth in you, live peaceably with all men" (Rom. 12:18). The apostle recognized that the balanced Christian has an adaptive capacity to exercise assertive, yes, even hostile behavior when it is appropriate to do so. Jesus' whipping the moneychangers and driving them out of the temple and His harsh words to the Pharisees are incidents that this personality prefers to ignore (Matt. 15:1-20; 21:12-17; 23:13-36). It is a bit jolting to them when they hear that justification of their extreme agreeability makes them come across as more spiritual than Jesus Christ Himself, who was comfortable with hostile words and behaviors.

Sometimes they will reply that Jesus could exhibit those hostile or aggressive behaviors because He was the sinless Son of God. But when they say this, they imply that the more they become like Jesus, the more they should be able to express aggressiveness and hostility! And that's exactly the point. This personality chooses to be the out-of-balance person he is, not because of his spirituality — it is a flaw of his personality. He is *afraid* to assert himself or admit to hostile feelings in himself. I often tell Christians who suffer from this maladaptive expression of personality that *they would be the way they are even if they weren't Christians*.

The tragedy of this personality is that he will see no evil and hear no evil even when brutally confronted with it. He gives

The Cooperative-Overconventional Personality

special annoyance to the Skeptical Personality, who sees hostility themes all too clearly and accurately. Leary, writing of the disastrous consequences of this blindness says,

> The rigidity by means of which these individuals can distort and misinterpret reality can reach astounding proportions. These misperceptions (sincere and not deliberate) can lead to disastrous misunderstandings. We think here of the patient who employed ... bland optimistic friendliness to handle feelings of despair so severe as to reach psychotic proportions. In the face of several catastrophic failures (loss of two jobs, threatened divorce), this patient insisted in the intake interview that everything was going well, that he was not depressed, etc.
>
> The discrepancy between the reality situation and his happy reactions finally emerged. The intake worker reviewed with the patient the intense conflict between desperate fearful depression and the cheerful facade. The latter operations were supported, but the need for treatment was stressed. The patient was delighted with the course of the interview, enthusiastically accepted the mild summary of the clinician, and eagerly cooperated in making plans for therapy, arranging future appointments, etc.
>
> Within two days the clinician received phone calls from three irate and puzzled people (his wife, his employer, and the referring physician), all of whom had been informed by the patient that "the psychiatrist said I am perfectly normal and don't need treatment." In a subsequent interview the patient remembered the negative or reality side of the clinician's original summary and stated that he had "forgotten" the plans for therapy and discovered the appointment slip which had been "lost" in his wallet.
>
> This patient was not a dishonest or prevaricating person. The rigidity and intensity of the ingenuous naivete, as well as the complete crippling of any other interpersonal reflexes, were quite evident. ... [such people] completely misperceive hostility in others and forget the occasion when they have been momentarily angry or depressed.[1]

The pastor and Christian worker who attempts to help such people is often taken to task for his own "unchristian" outlook on the situation and often exposes himself to kindly chiding by this personality. I have experienced this personality's dropping out of counseling, presenting as his reason that the counselor really wasn't the kind of Christian that he had imagined. Not only does this kind of dropout manage to preserve his unreal outlook on life, but he also manages to bolster his self-esteem by spiritual one-upmanship on the Christian counselor.

This personality tends to pull for support from dominant-affectionate personalities and others like himself. He tends to avoid those who can express hostility. The church presents the Overconventional Personality with the opportunity to feel as if he is a spiritual giant and to bolster his self-worth by calling "unchristian" those people in the church who have negative and depressed feelings.

Helen was a memorable example of this personality. When she appeared for her first counseling session, she wore a broad smile and appeared to have it all together. When I asked her what I could do for her, she told how she recently had become a Christian and then gave a glowing recital of the wonderful new life the Lord had given her. After listening at length I ventured the opinion that the purpose of the appointment was not to tell me how wonderful the Lord is. She agreed, and her face became more serious, though there was a hint of a smile as she presented her problem.

Before she was saved, she and her husband were "swingers." They regularly went to mate-swapping parties on weekends, but now that she was a Christian she had trouble with it. For a while she stopped going to such affairs, though she generously agreed to let her husband continue to go if it would make him happy. The problem was that no singles were allowed: you had to have a wife to swap. So her husband put pressure on her to go.

Hearing many sermons on submission, she concluded that she was making her husband unhappy by not being submissive, so she agreed to go with him. But being a true believer, she was troubled by the indwelling Holy Spirit, and it was this uneasiness that had brought her to my office.

It may seem that Helen was anything but "overconventional." But the Overconventional Personality is the person who takes cooperation to a maladaptive extreme and can do it because reality is blotted out. "Cooperation" is the byword — make people happy regardless of personal cost. And it is this that ultimately gets this personality into trouble.

The Cooperative Personality

Helen needed to make some behavior changes. Her extreme agreeability and continual smile gave the interpersonal message that she would cooperate at any cost. She needed to drop the following:

> Smiling continually
> Agreeing with everyone
> Overly eager to please
> Not expressing negative feelings
> Letting others have their way all the time
> Liking and accepting everyone without discrimination

The behaviors she needed to add were more assertive:

> Strict if necessary
> Firm but just
> Frank and honest
> Able to be critical of others
> Hard-boiled when necessary
> Stern but fair
> Able to express irritation
> Straightforward and direct

It was painful for Helen to look at the qualities that needed change. It was downright frightening. I was bidding her to a life style that she had always shunned as unchristian and dangerous. She was filled with a great deal of anxiety when I urged that she express negative feelings to other people.

In fighting this, Helen was frustrating the divine process of change. She wanted very much to have people like her, and she couldn't understand why her sweetness was not readily accepted. She was unwilling at first to consider that it is possible to be maladaptively sweet. If she really accepted this notion, she wouldn't be able to rationalize her security operation, and she would have to accept the idea that God didn't want her to be sweeter, but rather more firm.

Helen's obstacle was, she could not believe that the trouble in her life was the result of her supersweet behavior. She felt that the "unspirituality" of others was the problem and that it was others who needed to change rather than herself. She imagined that if her husband were saved, all her problems would be solved: but she had to admit that her husband was not the only person who created problems for her. Frequently in the church, people would get exasperated with her and tell her she was out of touch with reality.

It was natural, then, that when trial came, she found it difficult to believe that God was giving her an opportunity to change her maladaptively sweet behavior to a more adaptive form — that God was giving her opportunities to be more assertive. I pointed out that the escape spoken of in 1 Corinthians 10:13 was for her the escape of more assertive behavior. She could expect to continue to be hurt by her refusal to be assertive. She could expect others to hurt her deeply, and God would permit this until she exercised more assertive behavior — which would give her escape from the trial.

I repeat: God's method is continually to make maladaptive behavior unsuccessful through trial. When we seek an alternative, more adaptive response to the trial, He releases us from the testing, thereby reinforcing the changed behavior. When we slip back into our old maladaptive patterns, He provides another trial and again forces us into a more adaptive response, which then brings release from the trial and a reinforcement of the new behavior. *The pain of trial is God's way of forcing us to try more adaptive coping techniques.* When we under-

The Cooperative-Overconventional Personality

stand what needs to be changed in us, we are in a far better position to understand the purpose of the trial.

I attempted to facilitate the divine methodology for change by directive counseling. One of the first things I wanted to change was Helen's annoying agreeability. Whenever I began to say something, she would shake her head "yes" and say, "Uh huh; yes." She would do this even before she heard what I was saying. Whenever she did this, I told her how annoying it was and that she was not to agree with me. She was either to remain silent or disagree. And whenever it happened, I would play back the tape of our conversation and call it to her attention.

The other maladaptively agreeable behavior was her smile. I told her I didn't want her smiling at me all the time. Again she had a difficult time controlling this behavior. Finally I asked her to put her hand over her mouth so I could not see her smile or hear her agreement. The result was as expected: by the time the counseling session was over, she was tied in knots and exhausted. By frustrating her security operation of agreeability, I had created great anxiety that produced muscle tension and exhaustion. This did demonstrate, however, how committed she was to her security operation.

From there we moved into exercises designed to make her more critical. She was to pick out something about me or the room that she didn't like and to tell me about it. She replied that there was nothing about me she didn't like. I suggested that perhaps I ought to behave in an abusive way so as to give her something to dislike me for. She didn't know whether or not I was kidding, but she wasn't about to take the risk: she decided to tell me that she didn't like my tie. Though the criticism was innocuous, it was a start for Helen. I probed her to be more specific about my tie. The mild assertiveness on my part was enough to make her back off and tell me that she really liked my tie, and there we were — right back where we started.

I asked Helen then to choose something else. She hazarded a statement that she was afraid of me. This time I said nothing. We must have sat in silence for several minutes. When she saw that I was going to say nothing, she thought it was all right to go on. She said that my voice sometimes sounded stern and I often frowned at her. Again I remained silent. After many more minutes of silence she began to retract her criticisms and gave me a big build-up. Again I said nothing. She caught what she was doing and began to cry.

"There I go again. I can't even criticize when I'm invited to," she wept. Then with a frown on her face and sternness in her voice, she said loudly, "You scare me to death!"

With that I smiled, took her hand, and said, "Thank you, Helen. Welcome to the human race."

That reinforcement of change did more for her than anything else in the entire session. She actually was critical and confrontal, but didn't get slapped down for it.

I should not give the impression, however, that the Overconventional Personality is never critical or hostile. His hostility may not take the form of direct confrontation, but if the group to which he conforms is angry with someone, he can permit himself to go along with the group. In fact, he can be very critical of someone who is not present.

This may explain why some Christians appear so hypocritical in their behavior. When the overconventional Christian is with the person who is out of favor with the group, he will appear to be sweet and friendly. He cannot bear any critical or hostile behavior in himself in a one-on-one confrontation.

The second step for Helen was to enter into learning contracts with her husband and friends. Even though her husband was not a Christian, he could help her monitor her agreeable behavior. She wanted to stop smiling all the time and wanted to develop the ability to tell others what she did not like in a straightforward manner. Her husband was not so sure that he wanted her to develop the capacity to be critical. He liked her the way she was, which of course kept her locked into a sick relationship with him. Her Christian friends, who were perceptive, readily agreed to help Helen accomplish these goals.

The third step was the group. Jerry, the Distrustful Per-

The Cooperative-Overconventional Personality

sonality described in chapter 9, was in the group. Helen annoyed him no end: her smile and bland optimism became unbearable to him. Two hours into our second group meeting, he finally uncorked.

"I must say something to Helen," Jerry began. "Helen, I've been sitting here for two hours hearing others share their hurts, sorrow, and frustrations, and I've been watching you. You've been sitting there with a stupid smile on your face as if to say, 'Isn't that nice!' Helen, you're tearing me up with frustration."

Helen broke down and cried. She wanted to leave the group. The pain of the confrontation was almost too much to bear, but 1 Corinthians 10:13 came through for her again. Jerry, who was in the process of growth himself, said something helpful: "Please don't leave, Helen. All I ask is that you not smile all the time."

The Cooperative Personality is an asset to the church. This personality is well-liked and popular. Because he has the balance of assertive and critical traits, he is in touch with reality. The person with this adaptive adjustment is able to deal kindly yet firmly with those who would prey on the goodness of the church. He is able to assist in disbursing the church's manpower and wealth in a benevolent manner without being taken in by those who are not really deserving. In cooperative efforts he is able to get along with most people, but not at the expense of personal convictions or his own imagination or innovativeness. The Cooperative Personality gives the interpersonal message, "I want to cooperate, but not at any cost."

*The Responsible-
Hypernormal Personality*

Chapter 13
The Responsible-Hypernormal Personality

THE RESPONSIBLE-HYPERNORMAL Personality is another personality type that is close to the Christian and cultural ideal. This personality presents himself as a strong, self-confident, and independent person. But he uses these qualities in a loving manner. He wants to present himself as tender with those close to him and reasonable and responsible toward all.

THE HYPERNORMAL PERSONALITY

The maladaptive form of this personality, the Hypernormal Personality, is often driven by relentless ideals of service to others. Even nonchristians may have this quality.

It is extremely difficult to deal with hypernormal Christians. Their compulsive service, generosity, help, counsel, and support are usually interpreted as the fruit of the Spirit, both by themselves and by their friends. Though this behavior is often extreme and sometimes inappropriate, Christians are unwilling to talk about it. And when the Christian counselor suggests not only that the behavior is inappropriate, but also that it may be a device to cope with anxiety, he might as well be attacking God, the church, motherhood, the flag, and apple pie!

Jack, a former missionary who returned from foreign service to become a pastor, was just such a person. He had returned from the field with an ulcer, which was being treated at the time he came to me for counseling.

His purpose in seeing me was not for himself, he insisted, but because of his wife's behavior. She was "drifting from the Lord." After talking with Jack, I suspected that he himself was a large part of his problem, but I said nothing, awaiting further development of the case. I asked that his wife come for counseling with him, which she did the following week.

Pam was attractive and well-dressed, but grim. I could tell that she expected me to side with Jack and tell her to stop thwarting the work of God's servant. She unfolded a story of deep frustration. Jack was as heavily involved in his work as a pastor as he was as a missionary. She had hoped that when the family returned to the States Jack would spend more time with them as he had promised. He had said he was going to take care of his family and ulcer by reducing his commitments.

After a year of seeing Jack back in his old pattern, Pam simply gave up. She felt that if that's what being a Christian and what Christian service were all about, she wanted no part of it. She admitted that she had drifted from Christ, but she didn't care any more. Nor did she care that her indifference was an embarrassment to "Dedicated Pastor Jack."

While she was tearfully telling her story, Jack said nothing, but he obviously was pained by it all. Finally he said in the most loving manner he could muster, "But Pam, we're in the *Lord's* work, and you knew I was going to be a missionary when you married me."

Pam broke down completely. "Of course, Jack. The *Lord's* work! How can I ask you to spend time with me and the children? You're busy about the *Lord's* work," an emphasis she made with cutting sarcasm. "How dare I stand in the way of the apostle Paul as he wins the world for Christ?"

The Responsible-Hypernormal Personality

I suggested to Jack that perhaps his compulsive service really wasn't the leading of the Holy Spirit, but rather a maladaptive expression of his personality — a Hypernormal Personality, which I described to him.

He listened politely to me and to Pam's animated support from the sidelines. When I was finished, he looked at Pam with a condescending look as if to say, "You poor, carnal woman," and then he had some words for me. He told me that I certainly lacked a vision for the world of lost men, and it was no wonder that I "was no longer in the ministry." I didn't see Jack again, though Pam called and said, "Thank you for trying."

The Hypernormal Personality is poorly motivated for counseling, because he sees himself as fitting the cultural ideal; and if he is a Christian, he sees himself fitting both the cultural and Christian ideal. In group therapy he soon becomes the popular member of the group and is looked to for leadership and support from the "sicker" members. In interpersonal relations he most readily hooks into the Dependent Personality, and in a church situation he can be bled white by just a few dependent people.

As with the other personalities, the Hypernormal Personality is attempting to reduce anxiety and gain a feeling of self-worth. The church gives him a marvelous opportunity to do just this. He reduces his anxiety by cultivating the ideals of love and generosity in the church. He soon gathers a following that quickly comes to believe that it's not nice to make waves in the church and it's not Christian to express negative or hostile thoughts. The Hypernormal Personality tends to surround himself with bland, colorless people who present no threat to him. When those people are dependent and admiring, it gives him an excellent opportunity to boost his self-worth by helping them.

Though there is no standard psychiatric diagnosis that covers this personality, the hypernormal is a psychosomatic personality. In one study it was found that almost 50 percent of the psychosomatic disorders occurred in the hypernormal. The frequency expected by chance is 12.5 percent (Leary, p. 318). These disorders included hypertension, ulcer, impotency, and frigidity.

This personality is usually referred for counseling by a doctor, or he enters counseling to put pressure on other members of his family to fall in line. He asserts that the counseling is not for himself, but for the "sick" member of the family. This is what Jack had done, and this was the reason why Norma, another personality just like him, made an appointment.

Norma was very active in women's club work. She appeared mature and generous. She presented herself as a "spiritual giant," with modest affect.

Her problem was her husband — so she said. It was Jack and Pam in reverse: but my reason for mentioning this case, which was so similar, is the condescending manner in which Norma spoke to me. I like my clients to call me "Andy" because it seems to break down the doctor-patient barrier. But Norma called me "André." This is my given name, and I had no objection to her calling me André, except for the condescending way she said it. Sometimes I felt like a French *maitre d'hotel*.

One day after Norma loftily addressed me as "André" I said, "You know, Norma, when you say my name that way, I feel like a *maitre d'* in a fashionable French restaurant who is to show the fashionable Mrs. X to her reserved table." I suggested that if this was the way she treated her husband, it was no wonder why he was responding as he was.

That was the last I saw of Norma. When she paid for her session, she handed me a check with a grand benevolent flourish and said kindly, "Thank you, André, for your efforts." As she left I had the distinct impression that André the *maitre d'* had disappointed the fashionable Mrs. X.

My limited success with the Hypernormal Personality is somewhat troubling. I am encouraged to read, however, that the Kaiser Foundation Clinic in Oakland, California, finds that this personality stays in fewer sessions than any other type.

The Responsible Personality

I wish I had some grand success stories about how I have moved many a Hypernormal Personality to its more adaptive form, the Responsible Personality. Such is not the case. I am of the opinion that uninformed Christians tend to keep this personality from changing because the hypernormal seems like a mature Christian. For example, when Pam divorced Jack, she came off looking bad: How could she do this to such a dedicated, helpful, God-fearing husband? Only her close friends and I knew that Jack probably bore the majority of the blame.

Theoretically, in order to move this personality to its more adaptive form, the following behaviors must be dropped:

Overgenerous
Too kind to others
Always sympathetic to everyone
Too easygoing
Too accepting
Spoils others with kindness

I should note that these behaviors in a less intense degree would be ideal, but as listed above should be understood as extreme. The behaviors that should be added are the following:

Can complain if necessary
Able to doubt others
Able to express disappointment
Can be strict if necessary
Can be frank and honest
Able to express skepticism
Not easily impressed
Able to express hurt
Firm but just
Can criticize others to their face

It seems reasonable to suppose that the trials God designs for the growth of this personality will be designed to make him admit that he really doesn't have it all together and that his facade is just that — a facade. He needs to admit that he hurts and is angry. Such behavior brings balance and reality to the person with the I-have-it-all-together facade.

The trials God brings into this Christian's life are for the purpose of making him fall to his knees in humility and say, "God, I don't have it all together," and to make him admit this to those who are intimate with him. But he is afraid that if he admits he is not strong, mature, and loving, he will be rejected. And it is the pressure to maintain this facade that brings the hypertension and ulcers.

In moving to the more adaptive form of this personality, this person must be aware of what needs changing. He needs to see that what he fancied as works generated by the Holy Spirit were possibly generated by a compulsive need to appear spiritual and mature. Only then can he abandon his compulsive service, relax, and experience the delight of the Christian life in which Jesus' yoke is easy and His burden light (cf. Matt. 11:28-30).

In facilitating God's method of change — trial — the directive counselor would do well to handle this in a team counseling situation and with all the principals involved in the situation. It is easy for the hypernormal to single out the counselor as "spiritually insensitive" or "lacking vision." When more than one counselor and the rest of the family are involved, it is difficult for the hypernormal to label all of them the same way. He may use this rationalization outwardly, but he will find it difficult to accept inwardly.

Counseling handled in this manner is much like a small group, and it has the same effect — group pressure. Group pressure is not always bad, especially when it's in a Christian context. Indeed, this is what happens in the church when Matthew 18:15-20 is followed. The church is to be appealed to when the offending brother will not hear one or two people.

Learning contracts are an excellent way of getting the hypernormal to modify his personality. Whenever he is too

The Responsible-Hypernormal Personality

quick to rise to the aid of persons in distress, he must be alerted to what he's doing. He *must* at times be able to take a passive role.

Publication 525A of the American Institute of Family Relations, called "Suggestions for Clients Who Are Overly Active," offers some good suggestions for the person who would be more responsible and less hypernormal. It says in part,

> Take time every month to evaluate your activity. Keep a list of everything that you do for several days. Then go over them one by one, asking these questions about each: Is it really necessary? What are you trying to accomplish by doing it? Can you do it really effectively along with the other activities on your schedule? What are you afraid would happen if you dropped it? Considering it objectively, would what you fear really happen? You may discover some surprising motives for some of your doings. Weed out the ones that are unnecessary, either passing them on to someone else or abandoning them entirely.
>
> Be careful not to take on more jobs than you can handle. In clubs, learn to nominate others for the jobs. Refuse politely but firmly when someone nominates you and your schedule is too full to handle the job adequately. Don't ever take on a job when you *know* your schedule is too full, thinking vaguely that you can "fit it in somehow."

In making a learning contract, the contractor may tell family or close friends that he wants to do the above and may ask them to help him monitor his adherence to the plan.

Using group interaction to encourage adaptive behavior requires a sharp facilitator or group leader. As noted earlier, the Hypernormal Personality is soon hooked into a leadership role by the other members of the group who think him mature and capable. The group leader has a responsibility to the group to point out that the hypernormal is attempting to develop adaptive behavior, and this cannot be achieved by his being thrust into a leadership role in the group. This personality must be encouraged in the group to take a *passive role*, something very difficult for him. He can do this by refusing to dispense his "pearls of wisdom" and other forms of help, and by permitting others to minister to his needs. He should also be encouraged to express negative feelings when such a response is appropriate in the group.

The Hypernormal Personality who would become more adaptive can expect God to muster people and circumstances to frustrate him and force him into a more passive role. Only when he admits his frustration and takes a more passive role can he expect release from trial. As with other personalities, the pain of trial for him must be more severe than the fear of alternative forms of behavior.

Appendix A
Learning Contract

Date:

It is hereby agreed that ____(monitor)____ will assist __(the contractor)__ in learning when he exhibits the behaviors listed below by calling them to his attention in a nonattacking manner. These are the behaviors from the checklist in appendix B marked with "O."

_____ _____ _____ _____ _____

_____ _____ _____ _____ _____

(The contractor) can only reply "Thank you for telling me" when the monitor fulfills the terms of the contract, and he cannot explain, defend, or justify his behavior. The monitor is to call it to his attention whenever he defends or justifies himself. (The contractor) agrees to cease these behaviors when they are called to his attention.

(The contractor) further desires to develop the behaviors listed below. These are the behaviors from the checklist in appendix B marked with an "X." The monitor agrees to positively reinforce these behaviors by words and acts of appreciation when he sees them.

_____ _____ _____ _____ _____

_____ _____ _____ _____ _____

(The contractor)   (signed)

(The monitor)   (signed)

Appendix B
Interpersonal Adjective Check List

Please check those items which describe_____ NAME_____
DATE_____

- ____well thought of
- ____makes a good impression
- ____able to give orders
- ____forceful
- ____self-respecting
- ____independent
- ____able to take care of self
- ____can be indifferent to others
- ____can be strict if necessary
- ____firm but just
- ____can be frank and honest
- ____critical of others
- ____can complain if necessary
- ____often gloomy
- ____able to doubt others
- ____frequently disappointed
- ____able to criticize self
- ____apologetic
- ____can be obedient
- ____usually gives in
- ____grateful
- ____admires and imitates others
- ____appreciative
- ____very anxious to be approved of
- ____cooperative
- ____eager to get along with others
- ____friendly
- ____affectionate and understanding
- ____considerate
- ____encourages others
- ____helpful
- ____big-hearted and unselfish

- ____often admired
- ____respected by others
- ____good leader
- ____likes responsibility
- ____self-confident
- ____self-reliant and assertive
- ____businesslike
- ____likes to compete with others
- ____hard-boiled when necessary
- ____stern but fair
- ____irritable
- ____straightforward and direct
- ____resents being bossed
- ____skeptical
- ____hard to impress
- ____touchy and easily hurt
- ____easily embarrassed
- ____lacks self-confidence
- ____easily led
- ____modest
- ____often helped by others
- ____very respectful of authority
- ____accepts advice readily
- ____trusting and eager to please
- ____always pleasant and agreeable
- ____wants everyone to like him
- ____sociable and neighborly
- ____warm
- ____kind and reassuring
- ____tender and soft-hearted
- ____enjoys taking care of others
- ____gives freely of self

AP_____   HI_____   NO_____   BC_____   FG_____

____always giving advice
____acts important
____bossy
____dominating
____boastful
____proud and self-satisfied
____thinks only of himself
____shrewd and calculating
____impatient with other's mistake
____self-seeking
____outspoken
____often unfriendly
____bitter
____complaining
____jealous
____slow to forgive a wrong
____self-punishing
____shy
____passive and unaggressive
____meek
____dependent
____wants to be led
____lets others make decisions
____easily fooled
____too easily influenced by friends
____will confide in anyone
____fond of everyone
____likes everybody
____forgives anything
____oversympathetic
____generous to a fault
____overprotective of others

____tries to be too successful
____expects everyone to admire him
____manages others
____dictatorial
____somewhat snobbish
____egotistical and conceited
____selfish
____cold and unfeeling
____sarcastic
____cruel and unkind
____frequently angry
____hard-hearted
____resentful
____rebels against everything
____stubborn
____distrusts everybody
____timid
____always ashamed of self
____obeys too willingly
____spineless
____hardly ever talks back
____clinging vine
____likes to be taken care of
____will believe anyone
____wants everyone's love
____agrees with everyone
____friendly all the time
____loves everyone
____too lenient with others
____tries to comfort everyone
____too willing to give to others
____spoils people with kindness

JK____   LM____   DE____   DOM____   LOV____

Appendix C
Communication Workshop

What Is a Communication Workshop?

A Communication Workshop is a group sharing experience of twelve to fifteen people in which the members of the group are able to get varied reactions to their behavior, thought patterns, and attitudes on life and how they relate to others from people on their peer level. They discover through group sharing that their experiences are common to others.

The Communication Workshop provides a sheltered environment that tends to give the individual social stability, acceptance, assurance, guidance, and an opportunity for self-exploration and understanding in a sympathetic atmosphere.

What Is Expected of the Group Members?

1. All members are on a first-name basis.
2. All members of the group are accepted by the group by the very fact they are there.
3. The group leader (and co-leader if there is one) is as much a part of the group as everyone else. He does not enjoy "diplomatic immunity."
4. Everything said and done in the group is the property of the group. Violation of this principle will result in discipline by the group.
5. Every member of the group is committed to every session scheduled and to the full time devoted to each session. Each group runs from two to three hours once a week for eight weeks.
6. The group is interested in the feelings of its members as they relate to each other in the group and the manner in which they communicate these feelings. The group is not a study group, nor is it in any way structured.
7. A successful group depends on the honesty of the members of the group with each other and themselves. It is the re-

sponsibility of the leader, however, to be sure that the group always functions with the best interest of every member in mind.

Notes

CHAPTER ONE

1. F. L. Godet, *Commentary on the Gospel of John* (Grand Rapids: Zondervan Publishing House, rep. 1969), p. 294.

CHAPTER TWO

1. Charles C. Ryrie, *Balancing the Christian Life* (Chicago: Moody Press, 1969), pp. 47-48.

2. John Powell, *Why Am I Afraid to Tell You Who I Am?* (Niles, Ill.: Argus Communications, 1969), p. 167.

3. Harry Stack Sullivan, *Conceptions of Modern Psychiatry* (New York: W. W. Norton and Co., 1953).

CHAPTER FOUR

1. Charles C. Ryrie, *Balancing the Christian Life* (Chicago: Moody Press, 1969), pp, 9-10.

CHAPTER FIVE

1. James Dobson, *Hide or Seek* (Old Tappan, N.J.: Fleming H. Revell Co., 1975), p. 69.

2. Maxwell Maltz, *Psycho-Cybernetics* (New York: Prentice-Hall, Inc., 1960), p. x.

3. G. C. Berkhouwer, *Man: The Image of God*. Studies in Dogmatics, Vol. 8 (Grand Rapids: Wm. B. Eerdmans Publishing Co.), pp. 152-53.

4. Ibid.

5. Jay E. Adams, *The Christian Counselor's Manual* (Grand Rapids: Baker Book House, 1973), p. 91.

6. Ibid.

7. Cecil Osborne, *The Art of Understanding Yourself* (Grand Rapids: Zondervan Publishing House, 1967), pp. 25-26.

8. Ibid., p. 35.

CHAPTER SIX

1. The names used in this book are not those of real persons. The cases are composites of a number of people having the particular kinds of personality illustrated.

2. Carl Mundinger, *Government in the Missouri Synod* (St. Louis: Concordia Publishing House, 1947), pp. 41-42.

3. Ibid., p. 67.
4. Ibid., p. 81.
5. Ibid., p. 84.
6. Publication 510, "Suggestions for Decreasing Dominance," is available from the American Institute of Family Relations, 5287 Sunset Boulevard, Los Angeles, California 90027, along with other AIFR publications mentioned in this volume.

CHAPTER SEVEN
1. "The Pastor and the Other Woman," in *Christianity Today* (30 August 1974), pp. 7-8.
2. "Your Personality May Be Killing You," in *Reader's Digest* (August 1974); excerpted with permission from the *National Observer*, copyright Dow Jones & Company, Inc. 1974.

CHAPTER EIGHT
1. Everett L. Shostrom, *Man the Manipulator* (New York: Bantam Books, 1968), p. 13.
2. *Washington Star*, 11 April 1975.
3. *Unger's Bible Dictionary*, ed. Merrill F. Unger (Chicago: Moody Press, 1961), p. 552.

CHAPTER NINE
1. Timothy Leary, *Interpersonal Diagnosis of Personality* (New York: The Ronald Press Company, 1957), p. 273.
2. Ibid., p. 271: quoting Robert Lindner, *Prescription for Rebellion* (New York: Holt, Rinehart and Winston).

CHAPTER TEN
1. Russ Llewellyn, "Down With the Worm!" in *Action* (Summer 1971), p. 20.
2. Ibid.

CHAPTER ELEVEN
1. Edward W. C. MacAllister, in the *Journal of Psychology and Theology* (Winter 1975), p. 21.

CHAPTER TWELVE
1. Timothy Leary, *Interpersonal Diagnosis of Personality* (New York: The Ronald Press Company, 1957), pp. 309-10.

Subject Index

A

abuse, permission given 43
activity, too much 161
Adams, Jay 63, 64
adversity 51, 52, 59
affection 34, 35
affectionate-dominance 35-37
affectionate-submissiveness 35-37
aggressive behavior 42
agreeability 45, 147
American Institute of Family Relations 16, 81, 106
anxiety 29
anxiety neurosis 133
anxiety, reduction of 29
apology 79
apostasy 69
arrogant behavior 40
attacking behavior 104
autocratic behavior 44, 76

B

Balancing the Christian Life, by C.C. Ryrie 39
Berkouwer, G. C. 56
Betrayal of the Body, by Alexander Lowen 109
blunt-aggressive personality 42, 97-106
blunt behavior 42
bottomless pit 44, 132

C

call of God 75
Calvin, John 56
Christian ideal 44
Christian Reformed Church 56
Christianity Today 89
Christian vocations 75
clinging vine 44

common grace 55-57
communication workshop 126, 166
competitive-exploitive personality 23, 41, 85-94
contracts 61
cooperative behavior 44
cooperative-overconventional personality 44, 143-151
counseling, directive 59
cruel behavior 42, 104
cynicism 114

D

dependent behavior 44, 87, 136
dictatorial behavior 40, 79
disciplinary behavior 98
distrust 43
divorce and remarriage 69
Dobson, James 51
docile behavior 43
docile-dependent personality 43, 74, 131-140
dominance, 34, 35, 41
dominance, suggestions for decreasing 81
domination 79

E

efficacious grace 58
encounter groups 17
endocrine glands 27
endurance 53
exhibitionism 91
experience 53
exploitive behavior 41
exploitive, the competitive-exploitive personality 85

F

family, neglected 45

fault-finding 114
flattery 75
Freud 28
Fromm, Erich 29

G

Galen 27
giving in 123
Government in the Missouri Synod, by Carl Mundinger 76
grooming 91
groups 63
guilt-provoking behavior 98

H

harsh behavior 104
Hawaii, by James A. Michener 99
Hide or Seek, by James Dobson 51
Holy Spirit 46, 58
Horney, Karen 29
hostile-dominance 35-37
hostility 34, 35, 104
hostility, help for reducing 106
hostile-submissiveness 35-37
humanism 55
hypernormal behavior 44
hypocrisy 150

I

independence 91
insensitive behavior 104
Interpersonal Adjective Check List 46, 47, 60, 164
Interpersonal Diagnosis of Personality, by Timothy Leary 30
interpersonal relations 29
interpersonal theories 29

J

jealousy 114
Journal of Psychology and Theology 138
judgmental behavior 104
Jung 28

K

Kuyper, Abraham 56

L

learning contracts 61, 163
Leary, Timothy 46, 111, 116, 145
Lowen, Alexander 110

M

Maltz, Maxwell 54
Man: The Image of God, by G. C. Berkhouwer 56
Man the Manipulator, by Everett Shostrom 46
managerial-autocratic personality 40, 44, 73-81
masochistic behavior 43
meek behavior 131
modest behavior 43
self-effacing personality 43, 88, 119-27
Michener, James A. 99
mild pessimism 42
Mundinger, Carl 76

N

narcissism 41, 42, 86
neurasthenia 133
non-Christian counselor 45
nonaffectionate behavior 42

O

obedience 75
obesity 43, 109
Osborne, Cecil 65
overgenerous behavior 159
overgenerous personality 134

P

parasite 136
passive aggressive behavior 43, 109
passive role 161

pastor, autocratic 76
patience 53
personality types
  blunt-aggressive 42, 97-106
    competitive-exploitive 41, 85-93
    cooperative-overconventional 44, 143-51
    docile-dependent 43, 131-40
    managerial-autocratic 40, 73-81
    modest-self-effacing 43, 119-27
    responsible-hypernormal 45, 155-62
  skeptical-distrustful 42, 109-16
personality, adaptive 30, 37, 38, 39
personality, definition of 21, 27
personality, maladaptive 30, 37-39
planful, excessively 79
Powell, John 23
psychosomatic disorders 157
Psycho-Cybernetics, by Maxwell Maltz 54

Q
quarrelsome behavior 104

R
redemptive fellowship 65
rejection 29
responsible-hypernormal personality 45, 155-62
right, the need to be 24, 74
righteous indignation 98
rigidity 104, 145
ruthless behavior 91
Ryrie, Charles 22, 39

S
sadistic behavior 43
sarcastic behavior 98
Satan 52
Scripture 46
Security operation 30, 33, 111
seductive behavior 91

self-criticism 123
self-depreciation 123
self-importance 79
self-justification 79
self-righteous behavior 91, 104
self-worth 30
Shostrom, Everett 46, 100
sin unto death 67
skeptical-distrustful personality 42, 109-16
smile mask 131, 147
spirituality, definition 22
spiritual life, hindered by personality 24
spoiling with kindness 159
strict behavior 104
submissive behavior 34, 35
success 54
Sullivan, Harry Stack 29

T
temptation 52
The Art of Understanding Yourself, by Cecil Osborne 65
"The Pastor and the Other Woman," *Christianity Today* article 89
trials 52-69, 148
Trueblood, Elton 65
trusting behavior 44

U
uncaring behavior 86
unforgiving spirit 114
unkind behavior 42

V
Van Til, Cornelius 55
verbal abuse 104

W
warmth, nonpossessive 60
weakness 123
weakness, unbearable 87

withdrawn behavior 42

Y

Yokefellow Groups 63

"Your Personality May Be Killing You," *Reader's Digest* article 92

Scripture Index

Genesis
9:6 57

Joshua 74

Psalms
22 122
149:9 55

Matthew
10:29-31 122
15:1-20 144
18:15-17 64
18:15-20 160
19:9 70
21:12-17 144
23:13-36 144

Mark
2:23-27 138
3:1-6 138
3:13-15 138
3:17 105
9:17-19 138
10:13-15 138
10:20-32 138

Luke
6:35, 36 55

9:52-54 105

John
8:31, 44 69
15 . . . . 13, 23
15:3 18

Acts
8:13-23 69
14:16, 17 55

Romans
3:1 58
5 54
12:18 144

1 Corinthians
5:1-8 68
7:12-15 69
10:5, 6 68
10:13 52
11:30-32 67

Galatians
6:1 47

Ephesians
5 73

6:2-4 67

Philippians
4:6 133

1 Timothy
4:10 55

2 Timothy
4:2 87

Hebrews
12:1-3 66

James
1 80
1:1-16 . . . . . . 52, 53
1:5, 6 124

1 Peter
2:9 59
3:7 78
5:7 133

1 John
5:16 67

3 John
9 75